Sail

THE SURVIVING TRADITION

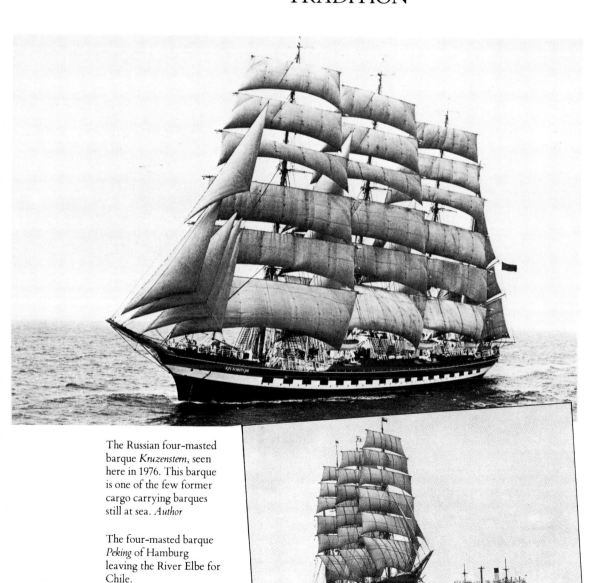

The Russian four-masted barque *Kruzenstern*, seen here in 1976. This barque is one of the few former cargo carrying barques still at sea. *Author*

The four-masted barque *Peking* of Hamburg leaving the River Elbe for Chile.

Aloft on the four-masted barque *Passat*, the watch are climbing down the topmast shrouds after having stowed the fore lower topgallant sail.
Anne Stanley

Sail

THE SURVIVING TRADITION

Robert Simper

CONWAY

MARITIME PRESS

Front endpaper
The wooden kotter
Wilhelmina, the steel
klipper *Aja* which was
built in 1910 as a single
masted klipper and the
steel tjalk *Anna Roosje* at
the Kromhout Yard,
Amsterdam in a pencil
drawing by Ron van den
Bos.

Back endpaper
On board the barque
Marques approaching
Harwich. *Author*

By the same author:
Over Snape Bridge (1967)
Woodbridge & Beyond (1972)
East Coast Sail (1972)
Scottish Sail (1974)
North East Sail (1976)
British Sail (1977)
Victorian & Edwardian Yachting from Old Photographs (1978)
Gaff Sail (1979)
Traditions of East Anglia (1980)
Suffolk Show (1981)
Britain's Maritime Heritage (1982)
Sail on the Orwell (with Roger Finch) (1982)

First published in Great Britain 1984 by
Conway Maritime Press Ltd
24 Bride Lane
Fleet Street
London EC4Y 8DR

ISBN 0 85177 317 6

Designed by Tony Garrett
Typesetting and artwork by Witwell Ltd, Liverpool
Printed and bound in Great Britain by R J Acford, Chichester

Contents

Acknowledgements

The Italian barque *Sant Anna* lying in Entrepot Dok between Amsterdam and Durgerdam in about 1905. This ship was built as the medium clipper *Edinburghshire* at Dundee in 1884. *Historisch Topografische Atlas Gemeentelijke Archiefdienst, Amsterdam*

Many people have been particularly helpful over the years and I would like to thank Norman Brouwer of New York, Peter D Albertsen, Annapolis, Maryland, Francis MacLachlen of Kingston, Ontario, Malcolm Mackay of Halifax, Nova Scotia, Alexander Nurnberg of Hamburg, and Ole Mortensøn of Rudkøbing, Denmark. I also want to thank Ron van den Bos of Amsterdam, for photographs and a great source of knowledge on boats, Geoff Cordy of Felixstowe, for photographic work and, most of all, my wife Pearl for her countless hours of typing and sorting out material.

R.S.
Ramsholt, 1984

CHAPTER 1

The Golden Age of Sail

It was gold which triggered off the chain of events which led to sailing ships reaching their peak of perfection. For the whole of the nineteenth century there was a long and bitter struggle between sailing ships and steamers to see who would dominate the trade routes of the world. Roughly half way through that century, 1848 to be exact, gold was discovered in California and in 1851 in Australia. The common factor between these two discoveries was that they were in new lands on the opposite side of the world to the centres of population. In the early 1850s 'gold fever' was reaching epidemic proportions and thousands of people were seeking ways to pay for a one-way passage to the gold fields. It was a ship owner's dream, but the public were in a hurry. The gold was only there for the first man to find it and everyone wanted a fast ship.

There had already been an elite band of sailing ships built exclusively for speed. These thoroughbreds of the sea were used for such limited trades as passenger carrying, naval dispatches and smugglers. The term 'clipper' was used to describe any fast sailing ship. Contemporary newspaper reports used 'clipper' freely as no doubt investors hoped this would attract freights and passengers, but there was never any hard and fast rule to define the clipper ships. Some of the ships described in glowing terms as clippers never really lived up to the title. Others, like *Champion of the Sea*, *Lightning*, *Thermopylae*, *Cutty Sark* and a host more legendary names certainly were clippers and regularly made long ocean voyages faster than other ships.

In the 1850–60s the clipper ships were the fastest form of ocean transport but every year the hated steamers (which incidently still used some sails) kept taking more freights and passengers. Steamers conquered the more lucrative ferry routes between the British Isles and the European Continent first, but the ocean-going liners (or packets as they were then known) were virtually invented for the North Atlantic route.

The very first of the new breed of liners (which ran on a 'line' between two ports) was Brunel's 3270-ton *Great Britain* which sailed from Bristol in 1843. Over the next twenty years other British, French and American companies established their places in the North Atlantic passenger services. Soon every maritime European country was sending steam express liners on this prestige route and were looking towards opening up other world routes. The process of steam replacing sail in passenger work went on over about fifty years and was followed by about another fifty years in which steamers took over most of the major cargo trades. Since this change took place over several generations, many men thought that sail never would die out completely. The clippers

This etching by Lionel Smythe, 1874, has all the qualities of melodrama loved by the Victorians, but the reality happened all too frequently. The crew of a tiller-steered schooner pump for their lives in a gale while the mate hoists the red ensign upside down in a forlorn signal of distress. *Illustrated London News*

came half way through this transitional period and many die-hard sailors regarded them as actual proof that sail could hold its own and possibly even recapture trade from the steamers.

There was no disputing that in the mid-nineteenth century sail still carried most of the ocean trades. The steamers had to keep going into port to fill their bunkers with coal. This coal was shipped, usually from South Wales, to the bunkering ports. Sailing ships on the other hand made use of the trade wind systems which were free. The deep-water sailing ships with square sails were ideally suited for running before the wind, although often many hundreds of sea miles were taken to stay with the trade winds blowing from behind them.

Sail was a practical form of travel, but when people were prepared to pay for speed then builders and owners went out of their way to provide this. The passages of the clippers were studied with great interest, not just by the shipping world, but also by the general public. Owners made sure that a good passage received maximum publicity because of the prestige it brought their ship. There was a record time for most trades, and some of these remained the same for years.

The British iron-hulled ship *Patriarch*, one of the clippers built and owned in Aberdeen by the White Star Line went from Dungeness in the English Channel to Sydney in seventy-four days. That was taking about a month off the average time for the voyage. Another Aberdeen clipper, the *Thermopylae*, covered the shorter distance from London to Melbourne in sixty-three days. These were real clipper times, but

The full rigged ship
Cromdale wrecked off the
Lizard, Cornwall on 30
May 1913. *F E Gibson*

The four-masted barque
Pamir has set her topsail
and is gaining on her tug
off the Humber, 1938. *P
A Vicary*

many ordinary merchant sailers took twice as long.

The most amazing clipper race took place in 1866 when four tea clippers sailed from Foochow on the China coast on the same day and two arrived off Deal within ten minutes of each other. These two were the *Ariel* and the *Taeping* and they actually sailed side by side up the English Channel, at times logging 14 knots. It was extraordinary that they should have come half the way round the world on a long passage round the Cape of Good Hope and still have been so close. The clippers were ninety-eight days, pilot to pilot, while the record for that passage was later set by *Elizabeth Nicholson* in 1868 at ninety-two days. The clippers often logged 18 knots, but when there was no wind they stopped so that even a fast sailing ship only averaged 6 knots on a complete ocean voyage. Even the *Cutty Sark*, which returned from Australia in seventy-one days, only managed to average 6.4 knots.

In North America the main clipper trade was an attempt to link the east and west coast via Cape Horn. For this long route between the two sides of the continent the *Andrew Jackson* and the *Flying Cloud* sailed from New York to San Francisco in eighty-nine days, while the *Northern Light* sailed from Boston to San Francisco in seventy-six days. These records round Cape Horn were all made in the 1850s in the years following the wild scramble of the Californian gold rush of 1849.

Steamers never did take this trade, at least not on the sea, because in 1869 the railroad tracks joined up across the United States and passengers quickly turned to the overland route which only took seven days compared to three and a half months of being cooped up in a little ship sailing round Cape Horn.

The year 1869 was a bad year for the clippers, for it was also in that year that the Suez Canal was opened. This allowed the steamers to take the quicker route to the East. The steamers of the Peninsular & Oriental Steam Navigation Company had already taken

The full rigged ship *Hutton Hall* at the Centennial Mill Company, Seattle, Washington in about 1900. *San Francisco Maritime Museum*

The Finnish shipowner Gustaf Erikson bought up unwanted sailing ships and operated them long after deep-water sail had died out in most countries. Here, in the 1930s, are the *Herzogin Cecilie*, *Olivebank*, *Viking*, *Mozart*, *Winterhude* and *Archibald Russell*, all ex-German and ex-British ships, laid up at Mariehamn, Åland Islands between voyages to Australia. *Ålands Söfartsmuseum*

the lucrative passenger trade between Britain and India from the stately East Indiamen, but then the steamers robbed the clippers of the China Tea Trade. The *Cutty Sark* was built in 1869 for John Willis, a Scottish sea captain turned London ship owner, with the intention of beating the *Thermopylae* in the China Tea Trade. In fact the *Cutty Sark* was too late for the tea trade and it was nearly twenty years later before she made her name as a clipper in the Australian wool trade. Commanded by Captain Richard Woodget, the *Cutty Sark* averaged eighty-two days in the wool trade on passage from Australia to the English Channel and her nearest rival was the *Thermopylae* which averaged eighty-eight days. The average sailing merchant ship took about 120 days on such a voyage, but

The iron British barque *Lady Elizabeth* built at Sunderland, England in 1879. She was one of many ships battered by Cape Horn storms and forced back into Port Stanley, Falkland Islands, where she stayed because there were no facilities to repair her. This is *Lady Elizabeth* in 1978, one of the most intact sailing ships outside a museum. *Hilton Matthews*

every year's average varied according to the weather conditions.

The clippers achieved their fast passages because they had long narrow hulls with very fine lines and carried enormous sail areas compared to their hull sizes. The clipper ship era began in about 1843 when the American builders started producing ocean-going vessels on the lines of the fast Baltimore clippers, which were usually schooners, evolved for smuggling and privateering. It was mostly American-built clippers that were chartered at the time of the Gold Rush to carry passengers, although some of the clippers which sailed crammed with gold-diggers were actually British-owned. All the American ships were wooden, but when the British yards started building clippers they turned briefly in about 1863 to composite construction, wooden planks on iron frames, and then to all-iron hulls. These all-metal hulls took the strain of the great pressure under sail much better than the wooden hulls. Most American wooden sailers had a short (and often highly profitable) career and then had to be broken up because their hulls had been so badly strained.

The true clipper era ended in 1870 after the opening of the Suez Canal but some fast sailing ships continued to be built, particularly for the Australian and New Zealand immigrant trade and for the fruit trade. However, improved hull shapes and better knowledge of stress caused by large sail areas caused builders to adapt and this allowed them to go on competing successfully against steam. It is a strange contradiction to say that it was obvious, in the second half of the nineteenth century, that sailing ships were doomed to extinction, but at the same time they continued to be built in large numbers and went on to reach their peak of development.

The sailing ships of the second half of the nineteenth century never really became faster than the clippers, but in order to survive economically they had to increase in size rapidly. The deep-water sailing ships became the bulk carriers on the long ocean routes particularly to Australia and round Cape Horn to the west coast of America. This was helped by having small low-paid crews so that the passage time at sea was not important, while the coal-hungry steamers were expensive to operate on a daily basis. In the 1870s most new square-rigged sailing ships were around 1000 tons, but in the next

In the Falkland Islands the condemned ships and their fittings were put to use. At Port Stanley in 1978 a capstan from a sailing ship is being turned by seventeen Falkland Islanders to haul out an ex-Baltic inter-Island trader. In the background is the 1856 wooden American packet ship *Charles Cooper*, the only complete vessel of this type left, being used as a warehouse. The Port Stanley warehouses are a unique collection of sailing ship hulls. *Hilton Matthews*

The Danish *Ellen* under shortened sail during a gale in the English Channel in December 1922. She is a bramsejlskonnert or topgallant sail schooner, because she can set three square sails on the foremast. Many similar steel schooners were built in northern Netherlands and Germany just before and after World War I.

decade they were 2000 tons and finally, in the 1890s, they were mostly over 3000 tons. In fact the trend continued with huge ships like the German full rigged five-masted ship *Preussen* in 1902 which was over 5000 tons and the five-masted French barque *France II* in 1911 which was over 6000 tons. But these large giants were an exception to the general rule and were built for specialized trades.

When the change over to steel hulls took place, Britain already had the largest merchant fleet in the world. The introduction of steel only helped to increase this lead because Britain was already a highly developed industrial nation. Shipbuilding became concentrated on the Clyde and north-eastern England because yards here were near the steelworks and coal pits. The steel in the hulls, masts and spars was far stronger than wood and was the reason that ships could increase in size. The huge steel four-masted barques of the 1890s were often called 'sailing warehouses' by the men who manned them, but their size allowed them (in favourable weather conditions and under alert captains) to make passages comparable to the clippers.

Because coal was mined in Britain, particularly steam coal from the pits of South Wales, it gave British ship owners an economic advantage to change over to steamers and after about 1897, when engines had become highly effective, very few British lines ordered any more sailers. However, even in 1910 Britain still had 19,709 sailing ships which was far more than her nearest rival, the United States, which had 7312 ships.

Britain also had the world's largest navy so the merchant fleet never had enough trained seamen amongst her nationals. British ships were allowed to sign on a crew of any nation, unlike the French which had by law to only have French citizens in service

The five-masted schooner *Inca* of San Francisco. She has the triangular 'sharp head' sail set right aft and the raised fo'c'sle head and poop deck of a typical West Coast schooner, while the multi-masted schooners from the East Coast had straight deck lines.

The three-masted schooner *Amy G McKean* about to be launched at Dartmouth, Nova Scotia in 1919. In the Maritime Provinces of Canada she was known as a tern schooner because the masts are all the same height. *Nova Scotia Museum*

on ships under their flag. The British ships were known as Lime Juicers because of the law that lime juice had to be issued aboard them daily to prevent scurvy. The daily ration of lemon juice began in the Royal Navy in 1795 and was one of the major reasons why its ships could make long voyages with its ship's company remaining in fighting condition. It is known that in 1782 out of the Royal Navy's 100,000 seamen, at least 23,000 were on the sick list, mainly with scurvy due to lack of fresh food. The introduction of lemon juice with Vitamin C meant that in 1805, although the numbers of personnel had risen to 120,000, there were only 8000 on the sick list and hardly any had scurvy.

The 1764-ton, five-masted centreboard schooner *Governor Ames* about to be launched at Waldoboro, Maine, in 1888. The men standing on the bow give an idea of the massive size of the wooden North American schooners.

The Shipping Act of 1844 laid down that lemon juice had to be issued on all British merchant ships, but in the 1850s most owners were (when they bothered at all) just supplying the far cheaper lime juice. At the time no-one was aware that lime juice did not have the same anti-scorbutic properties as lemon. In the late nineteenth century scurvy was again becoming a problem on both the Royal Navy and merchant ships. The lime juice issue was abandoned in 1927 and was replaced by concentrated orange juice when fresh fruit was not available.

The standard of victualling in French ships was much better and included a wine issue. Even this did not always overcome scurvy though. In 1901 the *Neuilly* arrived at Le Havre 148 days out from New Caledonia with half her crew down with scurvy. In 1915 the steel barque *Bidart*, bound from New Caledonia to Glasgow, was lost because most of the crew were down with scurvy. The ship was driven by a gale on to the Azores because the men were too weak to work the sails. French law tried to ensure that all French freight was carried only on French ships. To this aim, in 1881, subsidies were brought in to foster the growth of a merchant navy. It encouraged the growth of a fine fleet of steel sailing ships, usually looking very smart, painted white and further improved by painted gun ports. Any form of subsidy or restrictive practices, however, eventually leads to stupid waste; French owners, for instance, got a payment on the length of the voyage, so some ships made long voyages to places like Hobart in Tasmania before they even made an attempt to find a cargo.

Most European ships tried to load coal outward-bound on ocean voyages from either South Wales or the Tyne. This meant that coal was available all round the world and encouraged British owners to switch to steam. French owners, like the Norwegians, eagerly bought up many British sailing ships at very low prices when their owners went

Many types of working boats relied on sail power. This is the Norwegian sailing rescue ship *Svolvaer* in 1934. *Norsk Folkmuseum*

The Norwegian sailing rescue ships went to sea with the fishing fleets and stayed with them during bad weather. Here the *Svolvaer*, built in 1897, is seen through another patrolling rescue ship. *Norsk Folkmuseum*

over to steam. The firm of A D Bordes of Dunkirk bought many ex-British ships and increased their fleet to 44 ships, all sailers, thus making it the world's largest single fleet owned by one company.

A few British ships were sold to German owners, but this new nation was interested in developing its own shipyards so the majority of their new sailers were built at Hamburg. The German yards mainly concentrated on building steamers, but since their country had little natural supply of coal a few owners kept to sailing ships. These were owners who concentrated on trades which involved long ocean voyages; Rickmers, for instance, sent their ships to the Far East with coal and they returned home

The cabin of the Norwegian rescue ship *Colin Archer* shows the typical late nineteenth century fittings such as the oil lamp in gimbals so that it would remain upright, and the bunk in the cabin side. *Author*

Fitting out the *Colin Archer* on Malomya, Oslo, 1979. *Author*

with rice and bamboo, while F Laiesz's Flying P Line took general manufactured goods out to the west coast of South America and returned back round Cape Horn with Chilean nitrate.

Laiesz was to Germany what Bordes was to France, but Laiesz appears to have had active encouragement from Kaiser Wilhelm II and the feeling of national pride was partly behind the building of their two large sailing ships, the five-masted barque *Potosi* in 1895 and the five-masted 408ft full rigged ship *Preussen* in 1902. The *Preussen* was the only five-masted full rigged ship ever built and she was rather an unmanageable beast. The barque (which has no square sails on the aft most mast) proved a much more balanced rig for square riggers making long ocean voyages.

Germany went on building and developing square riggers long after other countries had turned completely to steam. These later German sailers were the peak of the development of the cargo-carrying deep-water sailing ships. Laiesz's instructions to his ship masters was 'My ships can and shall make fast passages' and his ships did make fast passages, often beating steamers on the way.

The Laiesz Line lost all their ships as prizes as a result of Germany losing World War I, but they bought most of them back. What is more, they actually built two new sailers, the *Priwall* in 1920 and the *Padua* in 1926. The Bremen shipowner F A Vinnen also built new sailers including the 357ft four-masted barque *Magdalene Vinnen* in 1921. By the 1930s even the Germans were abandoning their few remaining sailers and most of them were bought by the Finnish shipowner Gustaf Erikson of Mariehamn in the Åland Islands. Erikson bought ships cheaply and operated them on a very low budget, thanks to the low wage scale that existed in the rural Åland Islands. Every year Erikson's great four-masted barques caught the attention of the world press as they returned from Australia with grain for European ports. After World War II both German owners and Erikson tried to revive the use of square riggers as ocean bulk carriers, but apart from a few brief freights in the post-war boom, this was completely impossible economically. This unsuccessful era finished with the loss of the German four-masted barque *Pamir* in 1957. In the days of sailing ships, grain was always carried in bags in the hold, but the *Pamir* was returning from Buenos Aires with loose grain. When hit by a hurricane the grain shifted and the great four-master rolled over on her beam end and sank, taking eighty-six of her crew while only six were saved.

The wooden square riggers of North America faded away before their European steel counterparts. The American square riggers had a reputation for being very smartly kept and for their 'bucko' mates who used brutality to drive their crews on. Because North America had vast areas of virgin forest and few steel mills, both the United States and Canadian builders naturally remained very loyal to wooden hulls. In order to compete with the steel sailers from the Clyde, American builders turned out ships of the same tonnage. But in order to keep the longer hulls strong enough, they had to use a massive amount of timber.

The 'Down East' builders of New England fought a commercial battle with the steel yards of Europe. The main centre of building Down East square riggers was at Bath, Maine, where Arthur Sewall & Co launched some of the largest wooden hulled vessels. It is now a peaceful place and only its fine wooden houses and carpenter Gothic churches hint at that prosperous era. Just above the town is a patch of flat scrubland beside the wide Kennebec. This was the site of A Sewall & Co's yard and here they brought the building of wooden deep-water square riggers to its limit. It was here that Sewalls built the huge four-masted barque *Roanoke*. She had a keel 300ft long and was the largest wooden square rigger built in an American yard. Sewalls also built and owned the equally gigantic wooden sailers *Rappahannock*, *Shenandoah* and *Susquehanna* and of these Basil Lubbock records that *Shenandoah* once loaded a record 5300 tons of grain at San Francisco.

Sewall believed when they launched the *Roanoke* in 1892 that they had reached the

The bows of the brigantine *Sela* of Milford Haven in 1975 shortly before she was finally broken up. *Sela* was built in Prince Edward Island, Canada in 1859, one of many vessels built in the Maritime Provinces to be sold to British owners. *Sela*'s hull had been repeatedly doubled with more planks in a long career as a Whitstable collier. *Author*

The sea is the greatest destroyer of ships. Here is the brigantine *Luna* ashore on North Roads beach, Great Yarmouth in October 1980. *Great Yarmouth Press Agency*

A wooden hull does not last long once driven ashore. This was all that was left of the *Luna* the day after she ran ashore. *Author*

maximum size an all-wooden hull could reach. These wooden Down Easters were built and sailed in competition with the British steel barques. Most of these came from yards on the Clyde and the north-east of England and seem to have been quicker and cheaper to construct. In order to protect its own wooden shipyards the United States would not allow any ship built outside her boundaries to be registered under her flag. Like most restrictive practices, this was only partially effective since grain was loaded at San Francisco as cheaply as possible and this, in the 1890s, greatly favoured the British ships, although early in the 1900s the French Government gave a subsidy to their steel sailers so that they could afford to undercut both the British and American ships.

While San Francisco Bay lay full of ships of all nations trying to get a grain charter for Europe, the Sewalls living in the little town of Bath on the other side of the continent took the first steps towards steel ship construction. They actually bought the British four-masted steel barque *Kenilworth* which had been so badly damaged by fire that the repair qualified her to go on to the American register. Next, in 1894, they built the first American steel sailer, the four-masted barque *Dirigo*. She had been built of parts constructed on the Clyde and shipped over to Bath. It seems that Sewall also recruited a few Scottish shipyard workers and began a brief spell of steel ship building although their last square rigger constructed was the four-masted barque *Atlas* in 1902.

The wooden Down Easters were the pride of the American flag, but their heavy labour requirements and lofty masts with intricate sail plans made them too costly to operate. In fact it was the cargo schooners which were developed to compete with the steamers. The multi-masted cargo schooners were not particularly fast or handy, but they could make coastal and ocean voyages as safely as the proud square riggers. What is more, the rig on the multi-masted schooner was so simple that it didn't need highly trained seamen. Often these big American schooners put to sea with perhaps only the master and mate being professional seamen and the other half dozen men on board were just anyone hired on the dockside. Obviously such a situation was not ideal, but they could go to sea with a crew so small and unskilled that could never have set the sails on a square rigger, let alone reach a port on the opposite side of the Atlantic.

The 'terre-neuve'
barquentine *Capitaine
Huet* being towed in 1929
from St Malo, Brittany,
at the start of a voyage to
the Grand Banks.

Although resourceful sailors of the Down Easter square riggers and schooners
looked with a certain amount of contempt on steam ships, this later generation of sailing
ships would in fact never have reached their size if it had not been for steam power. All
relied on steam tugs to tow them into port; the sailers also were fitted with steam
winches, particularly the schooners, where they were used to hoist and handle the
heavy gaff-headed sails.

The whole thinking behind the multi-masted schooners was to make them as cheap
to operate as possible and throughout the nineteenth century multi-masters grew
steadily larger. There was then a large fleet of schooners trading on the Great Lakes and
it was here that the first possibilities for the multi-masted type were tried although of
course three-masters were already common. The first four-master was the 231ft *George
W Adams* built on the fresh water at Toledo, Ohio in 1875. She was followed later by the
first five-master, the barquentine *David Dows*. She was wrecked on Lake Michigan in
1889, by which time schooner building and trading on the Great Lakes was drawing to a
close.

However, builders on the salt water in Maine were now aware of the possibilities of
the schooner rig. The first four-master on the Atlantic seaboard was the *Weybosset* in

The Cancale bisquine *Aline* racing in 1926. The cutter on the left is one of a type which replaced the bisquine. Before 1900 similar luggers were used between Finistère and Flanders.

Egalité, last of the bisquines, ashore in 1978 near Lancieux, Brittany, where she had been abandoned as a motor craft. In 1984 she was being restored at Raymond Labbe's Yard, St Malo. *Author*

1880, but she was actually converted from a steamer. In the same year the 205ft four-master *William L White* was built at Bath. These early four-masters were given centreboards, but this was later found unnecessary and the practice was abandoned in the 1890s. By the time the last four-master was launched in 1921, at least 459 of them had been built in the United States.

All the time schooners were being ordered which could load a larger tonnage and in 1888 came the first saltwater five-masters: the *Louis* was launched on the Pacific coast at North Bend, Oregon, while the *Governor Ames*, built at Waldoboro, Maine, was almost twice her size and the only five-master to be given a centreboard. Five masts were the limit for the next decade, but all the time the leading builders were producing schooners a little bit larger than their predecessors. The *Frank A Palmer* launched at Bath in 1897 was the first schooner of over 2000 tons. She was also the first of twelve five-masters named after the Palmer family. The following year after *Frank A Palmer* came the slightly larger 2400-ton *Nathaniel T Palmer*, then two years later the 2600-ton *William C Carnegie*. Now in the final stages of their development the New England schooners had grown larger than the Down Easter square riggers.

In 1900 came the first six-master when the 2970-ton *George W Wells* was built at

Camden, Maine. Two months later the 3500-ton six-master *Eleanor A Percy* was launched by Percy & Small at Bath. There were only ten six-masted schooners built in New England. These great long wooden-hulled vessels were beginning to experience problems with hogging. Their tremendous length and the difficulties of keeping a wooden hull rigid made it almost impossible to stop them from sagging at either end. Yet Percy & Small went on to build seven of the six-masted schooners and lastly the incredible 3730-ton, 350ft *Wyoming* which was not launched until 1909.

The *Wyoming* loaded 6000 tons of coal, in fact more than the wooden Cape Horner Down Easters that Sewall and other Maine builders had built for the San Francisco-Europe grain trade. Even the Sewalls abandoned their loyalty to square riggers; they turned to schooners and produced the steel five-master *Kineo* at their Bath yard in 1903. The only other American steel schooners were the six-masted *William L Douglas* launched at Quincy, Mass in 1903 and the ultimate in schooners, the seven-masted *Thomas W Lawson* in 1902. She was the only seven-masted sailing ship ever built and loaded 8000 tons but she was so large that she couldn't enter many of the East Coast coal ports. Because of this she was eventually sent on a voyage to England and was wrecked on Bishop Rock in the Isles of Scilly in 1907.

On both the Atlantic and Pacific coasts it was very difficult to tell the American and Canadian (then usually still spoken of as British) schooners apart in appearance except that the Canadians were usually slightly smaller. On the Atlantic coast the Canadians used the term 'Tern Schooner' for a three-masted schooner when it had masts all the same height. The Atlantic schooners all had an uninterrupted deck line sheer, while the Pacific schooners had a raised white foc's'le and a poop deck aft. The Pacific ones also had a sharp-headed sail on the aftermost mast. There were, especially after the opening of the Panama Canal in 1914, several schooners built on one coast and sold to the other, but it was usually possible to spot their place of origin.

One of the main trades on the East Coast was hauling coal from Newport News or the Delaware up north to power the New England textile mills. Yet even schooners with small crews still couldn't compete with the steamers, so the schooners were reduced to barges and towed six at a time behind 190ft tugs. Also wooden schooner barges were built with steadying sails for this trade. The schooners had one last burst of prosperity when a speculative landrush in Florida during 1925–26 called for every available schooner to bring in building material. After this it was only a matter of time before the schooners finished. The last five-master under the American flag was the *Edna Hoyt* which was dismasted on a voyage from Cardiff to South America in 1938. Several four-masters survived into the early 1940s and probably the last one to make a commercial voyage was the *Constellation* which ran aground near Bermuda in July 1942. Many others were simply abandoned in some quiet shallow spot. The four-masters *Hesper* and *Luther Little* were barely twenty years old when left beside the rail track at Wiscassett, Maine. Forty years later they were still there, great empty shells with decks fallen away and all the timbers bleached white by the weather, yet the remnants of wire rigging still hung from the masts and some deck fittings were in place. It was also possible to see the square ports in the bows through which the timber had been loaded.

Even when steam was obviously finally winning the century-old struggle, the

PERSEVERANCE

DIEU ET PATRIE

supporters of sail still kept trying new ideas. The great drawback with square sails was that to stow them, the hands had to go aloft and out on to the yards. This made square-rigged barques very labour intensive and costly to operate. In 1893 Captain Farlie tried to overcome this problem by having two barquentines, the *Oberon* and the *Titania*, built on the Clyde. These had square sails on the foremast which were ideal for trade wind sailing on ocean passages and gaff sails (like the American multi-masted schooners) on the other three masts. The use of the barquentine rig seemed an obvious solution, but with only square sails on the foremast they were rather slow in the trade winds and in big seas the gaff sails caused tremendous wear on the gear, particularly mast hoops.

In 1890 several steel barquentines were built on the Clyde, all incorporating new ideas like standing gaff to try and make sail an economic alternative to the all-conquering tramp steamers with their long thin funnels. Some German owners stuck to sail with dogged tenacity and took up the barquentine as a serious alternative to the barque. In 1911 Hamburg owners had the barquentines *Mozart* and *Beethoven* built at Port Glasgow. In appearance these followed a rig which was widely used in the late nineteenth century, but a new feature was that they were intended to carry cadets for sail training. Even after World War I there was yet another attempt at producing a new kind of ocean-going sailing ship, when the German firm of Vinnens had five auxiliary schooners with square topsails on two masts built by Krupps in the early 1920s. These vessels had the best points of the square riggers, multi-masted schooners and even engines for calms and for entering harbour, but these did not beat the steamers and they barely kept up with the four-masted barques. Perhaps if enough experimental vessels

In the late nineteenth century there was a great boom in sardine fishing from South Brittany. Here are the 'Chaloupe Sardinières' (sardine boats) which are luggers, although the word 'chaloupe' became sloop in English. *Croland*

had been tried out, another rig would have been discovered. After all, the barques and full rigged ships were the result of centuries of trial and error. Serious attempts to evolve new rigs stopped in the 1920s. However, since the oil crisis of 1972 there have been numerous attempts to produce a commercial vessel making use of windpower through sails, but by 1983 none of these were offering serious alternatives to oil-powered ships.

When the golden age of sail finished most of the large deep-water sailing ships were either destroyed by the sea, broken up or left to rot away in some quiet backwater. Only a few were deliberately saved such as the *Cutty Sark*. She was acquired in the early 1920s by Captain Dowman who had been an apprentice in a sailing ship which had been overtaken by the *Cutty Sark* in the days when Woodget was getting record passages out of her. Dowman bought this tea clipper as an ageing barquentine off Portuguese owners and rerigged her as a stationary training ship at Falmouth. Fortunately the ship survived World War II and a society was formed and she was preserved at Greenwich so that the public can see a very good example of a Victorian sailing merchant ship.

The golden age of sail did not just produce deep-water clippers, it also created hundreds of different types of coastal craft. In the age of sail virtually every waterside village and town had its own type of local work boat. Many of these types were simply local variations of national types.

For instance in Britain in the early nineteenth century most trawling was done in (gaff) cutter smacks. These cutters were known as 'long boomers' because of the heavy spar at the bottom of the mainsail. By the mid-nineteenth century smacks from Brixham in Devon were roaming further afield in search of new fishing grounds. This meant voyages to Pembrokeshire and up into the North Sea. Long voyages further

The coal stove and enclosed bunks in the cabin of the Great Yarmouth smack *Heroine* built in 1859. It is very difficult to find illustrations of cabins and fittings of working sailing craft. *Ron van den Bos*

from home ports meant that fishermen needed larger, faster smacks, but the long booms of the cutters swung about so wildly when the wind dropped that they became dangerous. The trawlermen switched over to ketches, which had small mizzen masts which reduced the length of the mainsail booms. Ketches were actually more suitable for trawling. The gaff rig developed enough power to tow a trawl along the seabed and the ketch was better than the cutter because the mizzen and jib (sails at either end of the smack) could be used for balance and speed could be regulated 'over the ground'. To tow the trawl too fast meant lifting it off the bottom and if it was towed too slowly, the fish swam out.

By the 1870s most of the offshore smacks were ketches. The Brixham smacks had long lean bows and mainmasts stepped almost amidships because they spent most of their time in the long seas of the Atlantic, while the smacks from Hull, Grimsby, Yarmouth, Lowestoft and Ramsgate worked mostly in the short steep seas of the North Sea. To give them an easier motion the masts were stepped further forward. The ketches from Rye were smaller versions of the smacks as they did not have to go far from their home port.

Gaff cutter smacks remained popular in craft under 50ft in length because they were easy to handle and were fast. Some of the handiest smacks came from the Wash ports of Boston and King's Lynn. They had to be handy to be able to beat against the wind up miles of narrow channel. The smacksmen preferred tiller steering because it gave them a more direct 'feel' when sailing close to the wind. In the trawling smacks of 70–80ft they often had to rig a block and tackle to control the tiller in heavy weather. Even in cutter smacks the huge wooden tillers came up waist high to the men. In moderate weather a tiller was easy enough to control. The skipper of the King's Lynn *Nellie &*

A Banff-registered 80ft
herring fishing zulu being
poled out of the harbour.

Sailing once again in 1980
near Aberdeen, the 43ft
fifie *Isabella Fortuna* was
built for summer line
fishing in 1890. *G Coull*

Leslie, 'Sweet Tea' Norris, is remembered sailing along sitting in a deck chair with one hand on the tiller.

Fishermen engaged in drift netting and line fishing did not require the power of a gaff sail and they mostly used the dipping lug rig. The advantage was that because there was no permanent standing rigging the mast could be lowered at sea when the drift nets were down and this made the motion considerably easier. The great disadvantage was that when beating against the wind the lug sail had to be 'dipped' by the sail being lowered and man-handled round the mast on each tack, and then reset. In spite of this disadvantage the dipping lug remained popular because its lack of rigging made it cheap to operate.

In Northern France the deep-keeled luggers steadily lost popularity. By 1900 only the smaller fishing craft of Normandy and Brittany were luggers. However two ports, Granville and Cancale, which lie on the opposite shore of the Bay of St Michaels Mount remained loyal to the luggers right into the 1920s.

These were the famous 'Bisquine' which were perhaps the most spectacular French small sailing craft ever built. The bisquine were used for trawling, but they were very fast, particularly in light airs – a legacy of the days when their ancestors raided English convoys or made a handsome profit smuggling to English beaches.

From the southern coast of Brittany came the tunny yawls which were to France what the Gloucester schooners were to North America and the Brixham trawlers were to Britain. Until about 1890 Les Thoniers (tunny fishermen) were two-masted luggers known as 'Chaloupe Graisillonne'; but then deep-draught counter-sterned yawls were gradually adopted. 'Les Thoniers' had to be reasonably fast under sail to tow the lines through the water fast enough to make the tuna bite. Once the fish were

Resetting the forelug on Hobson Rankin's fifie *Isabella Fortuna* after it had been dipped, 1982. In fishing days the steam capstan was used for this heavy haul. *Author*

aboard they were hung head downwards in racks and these whole fish had to be returned to the port quickly to be canned. Since their season was through the summer, June to September, the tunnyman's great dread was the warm, moist south-westerly wind which turned the fish before they could make port.

The great Breton tunny fishing industry reached its peak under sail in 1935 when some 900 yawls were manned by about 6000 men. The main centres were Douarnenez, Concarneau, Etel and the Île de Groix and they were busy building new yawls until the bad season of 1936–37 started a decline. Then almost over night World War II wiped out the huge fleet of Les Thoniers. Of course it certainly did not finish Brittany's huge fishing fleet which is still thriving with very modern vessels, but those sailing tunnymen which survived that war were sold off cheaply. Of some 900 yawls which sailed from Southern Brittany in 1937, incredibly only about five were left afloat as yachts forty years later. In 1978 I searched down this rocky coast to see if any remained in their home ports, but all that we found were a few twisted and rapidly disintegrating hulks on the foreshore of Etel. On the North Brittany coast the fate of the beautiful bisquine was even more total, but there were rumours that one hull survived and after a great deal of searching she was finally located hauled up among sand dunes at the mouth of a small estuary. It was a moving experience to find this bisquine because even with the deck gone and the counter stern sagging, this was an incredibly beautiful hull. Under the counter stern was painted the legend 'Egalité of Cancale' and one wished very much that she could be saved and once again cut through the water under those towering lug sails. A few miles away the tourist shops in St Malo were selling every kind of memorabilia showing images of the bisquine, but strangely there was not the same interest in saving the actual boats. In 1984, however, this vessel was partially restored with a view to placing her in a proposed museum.

The tunnymen and bisquine of Brittany are almost gone, but the larger fleets of wooden fishing schooners and Grand Bank 'terre-neuves' barquentines were made totally extinct by World War II. It is true that the Grand Bankers of St Malo area and the Icelandic schooners of Paimpol had been declining since World War I. In 1895 eighty goëlettes (topsail schooners) sailed to fish for cod around Iceland. In 1929 this number was down to seven going to Iceland and four to Greenland. In Paimpol I was told that the last to sail was *Glycine* in 1935.

In the inter-war years as the Icelandic fishery became progressively less profitable the schooners and ketches were put into trade. Mainly this was taking pit props and onions from Brittany to South Wales. Because they had the fine lines of sailing fishing vessels they were a great deal faster than the average trading schooners. There was a kind of golden twilight era of French sail in the 1930s with these schooners making very fast passages. Two day passages between Roscoff and Cardiff were quite common and they rarely took longer than seven days. The 90ft (27m) topsail schooner *Oceanide* once made forty round trips in thirty months.

The ketches or 'dundees' ('Dandy' in English) were a little slower, but the ketch *Dixi* once made thirty-five round trips in thirty-two months. The *Oceanide* was the crack schooner which once sailed from Brittany to South Wales in thirty hours. This same schooner crossed the Atlantic – St Pierre Miquelon to Granville – in only twelve days which meant averaging about 200 miles a day. The achievements of the Breton schooners did not pass unnoticed as in 1932 the French Navy had two sail trainers built on the lines of the Paimpol Icelandic fishing schooners. *Belle Poule* and *L'Etoile* are painted white like their predecessors and have the same single square topsails which can be rolled up from the deck. Sadly France which had so many beautiful and fast sailing schooners, and luggers, had more or less abandoned its links with traditional sail although in the late 1970s interest in them was beginning to be revived again.

Of the luggers which worked around the British coast the most magnificent were the fifies and zulus from the east coast of Scotland. Like so many other working craft they appeared and disappeared in a surprisingly short space of time; they were only at their peak for about a couple of decades. The Norse tradition was very strong in Scotland until the mid-nineteenth century when the sudden explosion of the herring fishery caused the evolvement of the fifie. At first the Scots were very loath to abandon their open boats, but the loss of life was so high that there was great official pressure on them to accept decked craft.

In a way the Scots simply kept building larger versions of open yawls (Norse for 'boat') which they had been using. Around the Firth of Forth and north to Aberdeen the fifties, which had straight stem and stern posts, grew to be two-masted luggers of about 65ft (19.5m) long. A further development happened in the Moray Firth in 1879 when a Lossiemouth boat builder combined the straight stem of the fifie with the sloping stern of the scaffie and produced a craft which became known as a zulu. The zulus, in spite of being up to 84ft (25.2m) in length, still retained the dipping lug and general character of the small open yawls, and still lowered their masts and shipped the rudders inboard when they were drifting with the nets. After a night at sea, if the hold was full, the zulus

could get back to port quickly and when the two huge lug sails and jib filled they could make over 14 knots.

The fifies and zulus were the product of the great herring boom of the late nineteenth century. These great luggers followed the herring shoals down the East Coast to Yarmouth and Lowestoft and were great money earners in the 1890s. The revenue from the drifters created numerous little stone piered 'herring ports' all along the rocky Scottish east coast. The herring fleets gave the crofter-fishermen of Caithness in the far north employment while the west coast of Scotland became depopulated because there was no real industry.

Herring drift nets aboard the Shetland herring boat *Queen Adelaide* of Lerwick in 1923. Note in the background the steam driven capstan and the boom on the mainsail. The Shetland boats had zulu hulls, but a gaff rig, probably to make it easier to beat up Bressay Sound to Lerwick. *Shetland Museum*

CHAPTER 2

Training under sail

'Trained in Sail' and 'Sail Training' are terms covering different sailing ship activities. 'Trained in sail' applied to the days of commercial sailing ships before World War I when young men went to sea to learn how to handle a ship under sail. 'Sail Training' is a much more recent idea in which young people who are not necessarily going to make the sea their career crew on a sailing vessel for a brief period for 'character training'.

To the ordinary seamen before the mast there was not much training involved with their occupation. Most of them were from the poor working families and were obliged to sign on ship at about the age of fourteen or fifteen and picked up the sailor's skills from their shipmates. The hardships of life at sea quickly toughened them into men who roamed the world carelessly spending their wages on drink and women in whichever port they fetched up in. Those that survived the risk of drowning at sea and knife fights in the dockside dives turned into bent old shellbacks incredibly skilled in rope work and, after having to while away their time at sea, equally skilled at spinning a good yarn.

Many sail-trained men hardened themselves in coastal traders before going on deep-water voyages. Once such lad was W E Chapman who in the summer of 1899 joined the brigantine *Huntleys*, a Whitstable collier lying in the River Tyne, ready for the voyage south. The *Huntleys* was deeply loaded with coal and her ancient wooden hull leaked continuously so that the crew had to spend long hours working the pumps by hand. The crew lived forward 'before the mast' right in the bows of the brigantine in a dark, damp fo'c'sle. The food was plentiful but monotonous – one long round of boiled beef and suet duff.

The *Huntleys* took 10 days to cover some 280 miles to Whitstable and the whole round trip took 3 weeks. By the end of this time, W E Chapman had had his dreams of the romance of sail completely shattered, and for some time after this he did not get the urge to go to sea again, but in the end he set off to make a career in the merchant navy. His first really good ship was the American 680-ton barquentine *Alan Wilde* which was kept up like a yacht. In usual American style the accommodation and food was of a very high standard, and in return for this, continued hard work was demanded.

His next American barquentine was the *Glad Tidings* which traded between Baltimore and Rio de Janeiro with coffee. The Captain was a great crew driver and very few of the crew made the complete round trip with him. Chapman then went back into British square riggers like the Greenock four-masted barque *Lady Wentworth*, where the food was limited to the daily Board of Trade scale of a 'pound & pint'. British

The world's largest sail training ship, the Russian four-masted barque *Sedov* at Hamburg in 1982. *Hans-Joachim Gersdorf*

The Polish *Dar Pomorza* belonged to the generation of sail trainers which were built on the lines of merchant vessels. She is now a museum ship at Gdynia. *Author*

ships were known to be hungry but easy.

Another lad who ran away to sea was James Taylor who sailed in the British coastal schooner *J H Barrow* from Preston in 1903. After 'learning the ropes' on this schooner in the china clay trade from Cornwall to the Mersey, he signed on the barque *Micfield* from Liverpool for a voyage round Cape Horn. These young men all wanted to get on a ship bound round Cape Horn as no man could count himself as being a real trained sailor until he had 'doubled' Cape Horn. 'Doubling' meant rounding the Horn once, which resulted in crossing through the same latitude twice.

Many of the young men, like W E Chapman and James Taylor, who went to sea as seamen, were able, after the necessary sea time, to sit exams, get their mate's and master's 'tickets' and then get command of their own ship. Many seamen did 'come through the hawsepipe' to become a ship's master, but there was also a long established

The Danish full-rigged ship *Georg Stage*, built in 1882, has single topsails and only crosses four yards on a mast. These single topsails (second sail up the mast) were replaced in the new large square riggers of the 1880s by double topsails because they required less men to handle them. This ship is now the *Joseph Conrad* and since 1947 has been a museum ship at Mystic Seaport, Connecticut.

practice of apprenticeship, whereby parents paid a shipowner for their sons to be trained in the art of navigation.

The actual training of the apprentice was left entirely to the individual shipmaster, but most do not seem to have forced them to do anything. Becoming an apprentice was expensive. In 1875, the father of A W Pearse had to pay Captain Lewis Davies, master and part-owner of the full rigged ship *Cardigan Castle*, a premium of 75 guineas to apprentice him to this ship for four years. This was more than a year's wages for an ordinary working man at that time, so it was a considerable expense. For this premium, Pearse and the other apprentices lived separately, away from the foredeck hands, but they did menial jobs aboard. Since the captain's wife and family lived aboard the *Cardigan Castle*, the apprentices were made to clean the after cabins and make beds. This they bitterly resented, but they could not complain. On a bad ship they would happily have deserted in the first port, but the apprentices were part of the 'afterguard' and as such were expected to behave like officers and gentlemen. Moreover, if they had deserted their parents would have had to pay the owners for breaking their agreement.

Not every shipmaster used his apprentices as cheap labour, and some did spare time to help their apprentices. John Grier found such a shipmaster when he joined the four-masted barque *Bengaim* in London in 1906. Grier had already served in schooners trading between the Solway Firth and Liverpool, and *Bengaim*'s master, James Learmont, was a tough lowland Scot from the same background. Learmont had also started in his father's schooner from the Solway Firth, then had left to go deep sea and quickly rose to command a ship owned by J Rae & Company of Liverpool. By 1906 many of the most ambitious British shipmasters had gone into the better-paid steamship lines, but Learmont seems to have enjoyed the challenge of sail and made some good passages in an era when many British ships were little more than sailing warehouses.

The Danish training ship *Georg Stage*, built in 1935, although very small for a full rigged ship, has double topsails. Here she is giving a sail handling display at 'Maritime Ipswich 1982'. *Author*

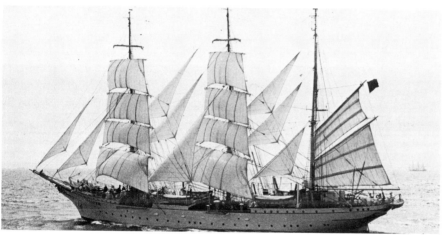

The Russian barque *Tovaristsch* was built in Hamburg in 1933 and like most German-built square riggers has the two gaffs on the mizzen to split the spanker into two sails. *Author*

Learmont practiced very strict discipline aboard the *Bengairn*, but this was done through strength of leadership rather than brutality. He did not force apprentices to spend much of their time polishing brass or scraping decks, and he trained them in everything connected with ships and seamanship. In the trade winds, when ships required little working apart from maintenance, celestial navigation was studied.

Grier stayed with the *Bengairn* until 1910 and about that time Learmont moved on to become a Trinity House pilot. In his book *Master in Sail*, published in 1950, Learmont told of his time in sail and record passages, while Grier did several illustrations for his work.

In some ways one can understand the indifference of the average sailing ship masters to the well-being of their apprentices. Most masters had received just the same indifference during their early years at sea and learning to 'stand on your own two feet'

The West German barque *Gorch Fock II* in the Solent at the start of the 1972 Tall Ships Race to The Skaw.

The Italian Navy's full rigged ship (frigate) *Amerigo Vespucci* in the Parade of Sail in the Solent in 1974. Although built in 1931 she is a mixture in design of the eighteenth and nineteenth century. *Author*

was very much part of the training for a career in sail. The cold hard sea treated everyone with the same total disregard. It was better to learn that early and stand a chance of surviving.

The age of British deep-water sailing ships ended such a long time ago that it comes almost as a surprise to be able to meet a man in 1984 who knew it first hand. This was Captain Charles Stone, a ninety-two-year-old sea captain whose cheerful and straightforward manner made him popular in the north Essex village where he lived in retirement. Charles Stone grew up in nearby Mistley, an estuary port, where his family figured prominently with coastal sailing barges. His uncle Harry had the ketch barge *Harold* while his father had the *Hetty* which traded across the North Sea and earned enough for him to build his own house on Mistley Green.

At fourteen Charles Stone had had enough of school and he pestered his father to let

him join a deep-water ship. By lying about his age and saying that he was fifteen, Charles Stone was able to join the 1900-ton full rigged ship *Latimer* in 1906. His first voyage was 152 days from Antwerp to San Francisco. The *Latimer* was about four weeks trying to get round Cape Horn. Three times the ship was blown away and they had to beat her back against huge seas to try again. It was a desperate hard life; most of the time they were wet and cold and the watch system was four hours on and four hours off. Even when below sleeping they were at any time at risk of being summoned back, with a cry of 'All hands on deck', to handle the sails.

The *Latimer* finally arrived at 'Frisco shortly after the April 1906 earthquake. The city was in ruins with people living in tents made of blankets. The ship was moved up the Sacramento River to load barley at Port Costa, then a Wild West town. After this the *Latimer* was nearly six months on passage back to Ipswich with the barley.

The *Latimer* was the last sailing ship owned by its London owners and after one voyage Charles Stone moved on to become an apprentice on the Anglo-American Oil Company's four-masted barque *Daylight* which had been built by Russell & Company on the Clyde and with her sister ship, *Brilliant*, were the largest British barques. The *Daylight*, built in 1902, was 351ft long and 3698 gross tons. Both barques were in the case oil trade between the eastern United States and the Far East. Tankers had already been invented by this time but in the Far East there were no facilities for handling oil in bulk. The *Daylight* and *Brilliant* carried oil in wooden cases, each containing two four gallon cans. The *Daylight* was in the case oil trade until 1921 when she was sold to become a tow barge at San Francisco. Even then her career did not end because in the shipping shortage in World War II she went back to sea with diesel engines as the *Tangara* under the Brazilian flag.

Charles Stone spoke very highly of the *Daylight* and the best run while he was in her was 109 days from Hong Kong to Baltimore. After five years he left the ship and returned home knowing that sail was really finished and he would have to make a

The Chilean *Esmeralda* leaving Auckland, New Zealand in 1966. She can either be described as a schooner or a barquentine. Like many purpose-built sail trainers she has accommodation for a very large crew so has high topsides. *Clifford Hawkins*

The Danish schooner *Fulton* was built in 1915 to trade with stockfish (salted fish) between Newfoundland and the Latin countries. She has been restored for the Danish Maritime Museum and takes parties of young people sailing in the summer. *Shippix*

career in steam ships. He joined the General Steam Navigation Company, was at sea through two World Wars, became master in 1924 and retired in 1957 as the Commodore of the Company's fleet.

In World War II he had been awarded the OBE and Lloyds medal for brave conduct and had reached the peak of his profession. Looking back, he feels that going off to sea at fourteen really deprived him of a good education, yet he had hated school and been crazy to get a berth in a sailing ship. At least he saw a way of life which was gone for ever in a short space of time.

There were many responsible people ashore who realized that the apprentice system needed improving. In 1890 the London ship owners Devitt & Moore, with the encouragement of the Round-the-World yachtsman Lord Brassey, started a scheme of training Merchant Navy officers aboard deep-water sailing ships. Over the next twenty-eight years they ran six sailing ships in the Australian wool and wheat trade, all carrying cadets and passengers. Most officers in the British Merchant Navy, which even by the Edwardian era was mostly steamers, had men trained in sail and they believed firmly that this was the way to begin at sea. One major shipping company, the White Star Line, bought the full rigged ship *Mersey* and between 1908–11 ran her as a cargo carrying training ship. However World War I ended Devitt & Moore's scheme abruptly and training in sail in Britain for men making a career at sea was never properly revived again.

In Germany there was a strong emphasis on strict discipline on sail training ships. Also the rough conditions of handling sails was looked upon as being a good challenge for young people. The Deutsche Schulschiff-Verein was started in 1900 and they had three full rigged ships built just to train young men at sea, but all three were taken away from their owners as war reparations in 1918. It was not until 1927 that this sail training association could get enough finances to build another ship, the *Deutschland*. The Deutsche Schulschiff-Verein is still actively engaged in operating sail training ships, but their square rigger became the stationary training *Schulschiff Deutschland*. The first

A study of Danish jagtbygget (yacht-built) sterns at Plymouth, 1976. The brigantine *Phoenix*, topsail schooner *Gefion* and three-masted topsail schooner *Lindo* were all privately owned, but chartered out so that they could take part in the Tall Ships Races to New York. *Author*

part of this name means literally 'school ship'. This was the name given to sail training ships before World War II to distinguish them from commercial cargo vessels. The word 'school' was also pronounced by sail trained men in a condescending way, implying that it was little more than yachting. These over-manned school ships only made summer voyages and they never attempted rounding Cape Horn.

However, sailing ships used for training ships do not sail under special conditions, and they have to face exactly the same hazards as normal cargo or naval ships. In theory the Baltic in the summer should be a safe place to send inexperienced youngsters, but the German training ship *Niobe* was lost there in July 1932. This jackass barque capsized when hit by a thunder squall with the loss of sixty-two lives. Undoubtedly this was a setback for the German Navy's ambitious plan to build up a fleet of sail training vessels. However they did have the barque *Gorch Foch* built in 1933 and then in 1938 her builders, Blohm & Voss of Hamburg, produced the Romanian barque *Mircea* on the same lines. They also built the *Horst Wessel*, now the American *Eagle*, and the *Albert Leo Schlageter*, now the Portuguese *Sagres II*, on the same basic hull shape. When history repeated itself and Germany lost her sail training ships after World War II, Blohm & Voss built a fifth barque to this design, the *Gorch Foch II* in 1958.

The German merchant service was also very keen to train its men in sail. The four-masted barque *Magdalene Vinnen* was built in 1921 as a cargo ship, but also had accommodation for cadets. The Laeisz Flying P four-masted barque *Padua* was built in 1926, very much as a cargo-carrying training ship. Cadets were helping to pay to keep this ship going and the following year Laeisz's four-masted barque *Passat*, a Blohm & Voss ship built in 1911, was also given accommodation for cadets. Laeisz continued to send their four remaining barques in the Chilean Nitrate trade until the early 1930s, but when freight rates started to fall, even the extra revenue from the cadets could not keep the ships at sea. The *Passat* was sold to the wily Finnish ship owner Gustaf Erikson while her exact sister ship, the *Peking*, went to the British Shaftesbury Homes. At this time British training organizations were not interested in

39

sending ships to sea, but liked stationary training ships. The steel Russell-built full rigged ship *Arranmore* was moored, unrigged, as the *Vindicatrix* at Sharpness. The *Peking* was at least spared having her masts and spars torn out, but she became the *Arethusa* permanently moored to a jetty in the River Medway.

In post-war Germany confidence in sail training continued for the merchant service and there was a last attempt to revive this idea. The four-masted barques *Passat* and *Pamir* were bought and fitted with auxiliary and were put back in trade between Hamburg and South America. This scheme ended abruptly in 1957 when the *Pamir* capsized and sank in the North Atlantic. The loss of the *Pamir* and most of her young crew caused a tremendous outcry in Germany against sail training, and the *Passat*, once she returned to a German port, has never been allowed to go to sea under sail again.

Nearly twenty years before the loss of the *Pamir* Germany had lost another cadet ship. That was in 1938 when the four-masted barque *Admiral Karpfanger* went missing with forty cadets and a crew of twenty on passage round Cape Horn from Australia to Europe. Ten years earlier there had been another cadet ship lost. This was the Danish five-masted barque *Kobenhavn* which vanished with a total crew of sixty while on passage from Montevideo to Melbourne. The *Kobenhavn* was one of only seven five-masted square riggers ever built and by all accounts this giant was superb. Everyone was amazed at the time that she could just vanish because she was fitted with a radio, but since then several modern ships with very sophisticated radio equipment have totally vanished. Usually with modern ships, an explosion is assumed to have been the reason, while the *Kobenhavn* may have capsized or hit an iceberg.

The loss of the *Kobenhavn* caused a brief halt in Denmark's very long standing practice of training young men for a career in the merchant navy in purpose-built sail training ships. The four-masted barque *Viking* was built at Copenhagen in 1906 as a cadet-carrying cargo vessel and the full rigged ship *Danmark* was built in 1932 solely for cadets, and is still sailing. However the 'Georg Stage Minde' (Georg Stage Memorial Foundation) appears to be the longest established training association because they built their first ship, the full rigger *Georg Stage*, in 1882. She was replaced with the present *Georg Stage* in 1935.

The interwar years saw a firm commitment to sail training in Germany, Denmark and Norway. For about four decades most Norwegian merchant navy officers started in sail training ships. The three major sea ports each had organizations which operated a sail training ship. At Bergen on the west coast there was the barque *Statsraad Lehmkuhl* while right down on the southern tip of Norway the full rigged ship *Sørlandet* sailed from Kristiansand. Another equally attractive full rigger, the *Christian Radich* was, and still is, based at Oslo. Since the safety record of the Norwegian merchant navy has in recent times been very high it is assumed that these preparatory sail training schemes have been successful. However the expense of maintaining three square riggers meant that by the 1970s only the *Christian Radich* was still sailing regularly.

These smart white-hulled Norwegian sail trainers were purpose-built and did not attempt to carry cargoes. In the interwar years this was a very new idea for the

One of *Marques'* crew splicing on her foretop yard. *Author*

Young trainees aboard the barque *Marques* during the Round Britain Clipper Challenge Race with *Ciudad De Inca* in 1982. The *Marques*, together with eighteen of her crew, was lost in June 1984 during the Tall Ships Race. *Author*

merchant service. But an even more radical approach was that of an individually-owned square rigger offering passages at sea. This happened in 1936 when Alan Villiers bought the Danish training ship *Georg Stage*, renamed her *Joseph Conrad* and sailed round the world with cadets.

For over forty years Alan Villiers was the best known personality in the world on square riggers. He was born in Melbourne in 1903 and was determined to go into the merchant navy in sailing ships. Just after World War I he signed on the barque *Rothsay*, one of the little square riggers still active in the inter-colonial trade in Australia. Later Villiers became a seaman on the Finnish barque *Lawhill* for a voyage round Cape Horn to Europe, but with square riggers being broken up all over the world, he left the sea and became a journalist in Tasmania. In 1928 he joined the four-masted barque *Herzogin Cecilie* and wrote a highly successful book *Falmouth for Orders* about a race with the Swedish barque *Beatrice* from Australia to Falmouth with grain.

With money from his writing Villiers became part owner of the barque *Parma* in 1931 and began to write a long series of books about his experiences in square riggers. The voyage of the *Joseph Conrad*, apart from fulfilling Villiers' ambition of commanding a square rigger round Cape Horn, was part of his one-man crusade to train men in sail. After World War II in which he rose to a commander and commanded a landing craft in the Normandy Landing, Villiers briefly became master of the Outward Bound Sea School ketch *Warspite*. But he did not really fit in with the new form of sail training for young people, for he really wanted the traditional form of training in sail to continue. Villiers actively fostered the belief that only men trained in sail could handle a square rigger. Had this been true the growth in the number of square riggers in recent decades could not have taken place. However, what Villiers did do through his excellent writing was to found a bridge by which knowledge from the old era of sail could be transmitted to later generations who have started to build and sail traditional sailing ships all over again.

A modern sail training ship is enormously expensive to build and operate because two sets of propulsion, sail and power, have to be maintained in perfect condition. To overcome this problem the Scandinavians built quite small ships – the 205ft *Christian Radich* is only 207 tons net – but their size limits the number of cadets they can carry. The stature of the cadets can also mean a ship has to be scaled down. For instance, the Japanese sail training barques *Nippon Maru* and *Kaiwo Maru* are 743 tons net, rigged as four-masters, but are much smaller than, say, the *Passat* because the Japanese are much smaller than Europeans.

The building of square riggers for training is such a heavy capital outlay that in most cases only governments can afford to commission such ships. Governments often build sail training ships with an eye to their being prestige symbols in foreign ports. The 301ft full rigged ship *Libertad*, which at one stage was the world's largest square rigger in commission, was built in Argentina in 1960 and is very much a source of national prestige when on long cruises visiting ports all over the world. She is also a fast ship for in 1967 on passage from Nova Scotia to Ireland she logged 1335 miles in 124 hours which meant averaging about 10 knots under sail. However in 1972 some of her crew told me that in order to keep up with her schedule *Libertad* only sailed with a fair wind and at other times she relied on her engines which gave about 13 knots. The emphasis aboard was on naval training rather than sail training. There was little attempt to use all the energy of the huge 380-strong crew for each mast had two powered capstans for handling the sails and when under power only ten people were needed on deck.

Both Portugal and Spain maintain large sail trainers in the form of the barque *Sagres II* and the four-masted schooner *Juan Sebastian De Elcano* and the Latin American countries which have no long-standing tradition of large sail training ships have followed suit. The Chileans have the *Esmeralda*, a sister ship to the Spanish schooner, the Argentines have the *Libertad* which they built themselves, while other Latin American countries have all gone to one Spanish yard for new ships. This is the Astilleros Celaya at Bilbao which in 1968 built the 250ft *Gloria* for the Colombian Navy. She was followed by the *Guayas* for Ecuador in 1976, *Simon Bolivar* for

The Polish schooner *Zawisza Czarny* (Black Knight) was built as a fishing vessel in 1951 and converted later to a Sea Cadet training ship. *Author*

Venzuela in 1980 and the largest of the Senermar-designed barques from Bilbao, the 295ft *Cuauhtémoc*, in 1981 for the Mexican Navy and named after the last Aztec emperor who succeeded Montezuma.

Most countries can only afford to run one square-rigged sail trainer, but Russia has several, most of these being seized from Germany at the end of World War II. The largest of these were the four-masted barques *Magdalene Vinnen* and *Padua* which became *Sedov* and *Kruzenstern*. The Soviet authorities have always been notoriously secretive about these vessels although both were seen at sea during the 1960s. In 1974 the Tall Ships Race started behind the Iron Curtain, for the first time, at Gdynia in Poland and this resulted in the *Kruzenstern* and *Tovaristsch* (ex-*Gorch Fock*) visiting western ports.

In 1976 the *Kruzenstern* and *Tovaristsch* again took part in the Tall Ships Race and visited Plymouth. The *Kruzenstern* was operated by the Soviet Ministry of Fisheries from Riga in the Baltic, making four cruises a year with trainees. The *Tovaristsch* was a naval training ship commanded by Captain Oleg Pavlovich Vandenko with a crew of 190. Both ships were in very good order although the cadets did not mix freely with people ashore. The atmosphere on the Soviet ships was extremely formal while on the Polish full rigged ship *Dar Pomorza* it was completely different. On the Polish ship there were strains of pop music coming from below and everyone was very relaxed. This was apparently the last voyage the *Dar Pomorza* made with Captain K Jurkewick in command. He had joined the ship in 1931 and became master in 1953. The *Dar Pomorza*, built as the German *Princess Eitel Friedrich* in 1909, was then the oldest sail training ship and did not finally withdraw from active service until 1981 when she became a museum ship at Gdynia.

The 56ft British owned gaff ketch *Angele Aline*, built as a fishing vessel at Fécamp, France in 1921, with the Polish ship *Dar Mlodziezy* leaving St Malo for the start of the Tall Ships Races to Canada and back to Liverpool, 1984. *Author*

The Russians withdrew the *Tovaristsch* from sea duty just before this, apparently because her hull was showing signs of age. In 1981 the four-masted barque *Sedov* was back in commission visiting western ports. A particularly hospitable visit was made to Hamburg in 1982 when many former German crew members were welcomed aboard. *Sedov* is by far the world's largest sailing ship, being 319ft long, 3545 gross tons and setting 45,122sq ft of sail. She easily dwarfs the large sailers like *Kruzenstern* and *Libertad*.

Some nations maintain sail training ships at a low key such as the Royal Netherlands Navy. The Naval College at Nieuwediep had the corvette *Urania* built in 1867 and until 1908 she made training voyages on the Zuiderzee. She was only about 90ft long but was rigged as a full rigged ship with a deep single topsail typical of a warship of the early and mid-nineteenth century. *Urania* was shoal draft and specially designed for the shallow Zuiderzee. In recent years the Royal Netherlands Navy has had the ketch *Urania* which is sailed with cadets from Den Helder, but this is a small part of their training.

The British Royal Navy sent many of its officers and ratings under sail for part of their training in the nineteenth century. This was done in brigs attached to training ships and there were also Flying Squadrons which made deep-water cruises to instruct young officers and men in seamanship. The squadron all had steam engines, but made passages under sail. The flying squadrons survived the loss of two ships, *Eurydice* in a squall off the Isle of Wight in 1878 and *Atalanta* in the North Atlantic in 1880, but nearly twenty years later it was strongly argued that there was little point in training men to handle sails if they were going to spend their time in steam warships. The Royal Navy abandoned training in sail and the last ship to fly the broad pennant of the Flying Squadron, before it was disbanded in 1899, was the iron frigate *Raleigh*. She was probably the last square rigger in the Royal Navy to double Cape Horn under canvas.

The French Navy's training topsail schooner *Belle Poule. Author*

In Britain merchant navy training in sail ended during World War I when Devitt & Moore's barque was stopped. Ever since then there has been a lobby of opinion in Britain trying to get some form of square rigger sailing under the red ensign. Although no official government department has ever shown any real sign of returning to sail, a whole series of schemes have been started.

Most training of young men was done from moored training ships such as the *Conway* in the Menai Straits and the *Worcester* in the Thames, but C C Graham, the Mayor of Scarborough, started a sea training school in 1916 which placed great emphasis on actual experience at sea. In 1924 this Scarborough school bought an ex-Bristol Channel pilot cutter and then two years later a 78ft pilot schooner built at Bremerhaven in 1878, which became first the *Maisie Graham* and then later the Outward Bound School's *Prince Louis*. This schooner sailed out of Burghead on the Moray Firth and was replaced in 1955 by a three-masted Baltic trading schooner *Peder Most* which became the *Prince Louis II*. The Outward Bound School was not primarily interested in sail training, but just included the schooner in its programme of adventure training. In 1967 the *Prince Louis II* was sold and the Outward Bound School concentrated on sailing smaller craft.

The lobby in Britain which urged for some kind of sail training vessel received a great deal of public sympathy during the 'Operation Sail' rally in New York in 1964 because there was no large British ship present. The Sail Training Association was running a campaign to raise money to build their own vessel for adventure sail training and this was made easier because the Outward Bound school had already proved the worth of this form of experience under sail for young people. This lead to the Sail Training Association having the three-masted topsail schooner *Sir Winston Churchill* built, which was a disappointment to many traditional sail supporters. The *Sir Winston*

Churchill is basically a large yacht belonging to the same line of development as the three-masted schooner yacht *Creole* which British cadets sailed on in the first Tall Ships Race. It is not surprising that the *Churchill* should have caused a few raised eyebrows. She was the first of a new type of vessel purpose built for adventure sail training. She proved to be highly popular and was followed by the *Malcolm Miller* which has slightly less beam. At sea it is often difficult to tell them apart, except that the *Miller* has straight tops to her deck house doors while those on the *Churchill* are rounded.

In 1971 the traditionalists got a ship to their liking when the Dulverton Trust had the 104ft three-masted topgallant schooner *Captain Scott* built of wood in a yard at Buckie, which normally built fishing boats. While most ship-building yards in Britain had switched to steel or GRP the good supply of local timber had enabled the progressive fishing industry on the north east coast of Scotland to keep to wooden hulls. The *Captain Scott* had the look of a trading schooner above water, but her underwater lines of a yacht seem to have given her a cutaway forefoot. This was reported to have made her difficult to tack because of the lack of grip on the water needed for the three square sails. The square sails on British topsails schooners were their 'insurance policy' against failing to tack in a seaway. The topsails could be abacked to force the head round on to another tack. The main reason for using a traditionally rigged vessel for sail training is that they require a lot of labour to handle the sails, especially to stow the sails when the crew has to go aloft and out on to the yards. This is exactly the opposite to the working sailing vessels who tried to cut down on the number of crew in order to operate more cheaply.

Generally speaking adventure sail training vessels tend to be a blend of traditional appearance and modern yacht design. One of the first ventures in this type of vessel was master-minded by Canadian marine engineer Francis MacLachlan of Kingston, Ontario, who in 1953 designed the brigantine *St Lawrence II*. A group of volunteers at Kingston raised the money and built *St Lawrence II* and she began sailing on Lake Ontario in 1957. Since then two more sister ships have been built for sailing on these freshwater Great Lakes.

The Canadian brigantines can be sailed in strong winds under staysail, like a fore-and-aft schooner. The same is true of the Sea Cadet Corp's brig *Royalist*, but keeping alive the art of handling a traditional sailing vessel is only a by-product of sail training. The real purpose is giving young people a chance to experience a challenge they would not normally meet in life ashore. In that they are entirely successful.

CHAPTER 3

Ocean voyages for adventure

The old sailors, known as shellbacks after decades of hard living and heavy work, used to say that men who went to sea for enjoyment would go to hell for pleasure. The shellbacks went to sea because they had no other way of earning a living, while people who undertake modern voyages in sail do so to expand their experiences of life.

The curiosity to know what lies just over the horizon was the motive which drove mankind on to explore the world. All the great explorers endured hardship and often died just trying to satisfy their curiousity as to what lay just round the next headland or over the next range of mountains. In time most of the world's surface was visited and mapped, but the desire of each individual to see and experience the unknown has remained just as strong. In Victorian times yachts were already making long voyages and often potentially dangerous cruises into areas such as the Arctic but these were manned by professional crews with the owner and his guests continuing to have the extension of their priviledged life ashore. The true adventure voyages began in the 1930s when people of modest income moved heaven and earth to finance long voyages

The British barquentine *Cap Pilar* arriving at New York in 1938 on a round-the-world adventure voyage. She was built in 1911 as a St Malo Grand Banker and was broken up at Wivenhoe, Essex in about 1965. *Mariners Museum, Newport News*

Some of the crew of the Norwegian barquentine *Regina Maris* in 1969. On the right is Paul Maskell who stayed with the ship and became her master in the Pacific charter work. *J & S Wilson*

The barquentine *Regina Maris* in the ice at Kristiansand, Norway, 36 hours before she sailed on 13 February 1970 for Australia. *J & S Wilson*

in comparatively large sailing vessels.

Three ventures of this period made a lasting impact due to the publicity they received and the fact that books were later published about them. Firstly came Alan Villiers, who had left his native Australia to make voyages as a seaman in the last European barques in the grain trade and before beginning a career as a journalist. Later he became part owner of the four-masted barque *Parma* in the grain trade, but then he bought the Danish training ship *Georg Stage*, renamed her *Joseph Conrad* and made a round-the-world voyage. Villiers ran his ships with all the strict discipline and some of the prejudices of the old Cape Horn sailors. During the *Joseph Conrad*'s voyage Alan Villiers proved his ability as a sailing ship master and overcame some tough problems, but this was to have been the beginning of a sail training venture and that didn't succeed. The old style of seafaring could not be transplanted into a more democratic age.

One of the greatest problems any ship on a long voyage has to overcome is that of personality clashes and strict discipline is one way of making sure the ship and crew stays together as a working unit. Sulks and strikes are a luxury that only a land-based community can afford; at sea they are simply not feasible. A very different approach to the *Joseph Conrad*'s style of management was made by Adrian Seligman in the barquentine *Cap Pilar*. He described it as 'an adventure in living. At a time when nations and classes, continents and races, were at loggerheads we set out – not to escape from the catastrophe which everyone knew must soon result, but to find out for ourselves, free from press and radio propaganda, from the prejudice of friends and the malice of enemies, if young people of widely differing types and nationalities could live at peace and achieve something together.'

This then was beginning a new approach to adventure voyages and also a very real understanding of how important it was going to be for all nations to find some way of living together in peace. The *Cap Pilar* was a French Grand Bank cod fisher, built in 1911 and fitted out at St Malo in 1936 for her world voyage. Each member of her crew paid £100 and the *Cap Pilar* sailed from an England pre-occupied with not getting involved in the Spanish Civil War and two years later dropped anchor in Falmouth as gas masks were being given out at the time of the Munich Crisis. The *Cap Pilar* spent the rest of her career moored to a wharf at Wivenhoe, Essex, quietly decaying away. I remember seeing her there with the spars still aloft and most of the timber bleached white by the weather. The achievement made by *Cap Pilar* was that it gave the crew a chance to get life into perspective away from continual political crisis.

The third venture or rather series of ventures were the voyages of Americans Irving and Electra Johnson. Irving Johnson had sailed in the Finnish four-masted barque *Peking* round Cape Horn and in 1933 with his brother bought a wooden German pilot schooner and after renaming her *Yankee* sailed round the world three times in eight years. After World War II Irving Johnson bought a steel German pilot schooner, again renamed her *Yankee* and after altering her to a brigantine was soon off round the world again carrying crews of young people. After this he had designed for him a cruising yacht, another *Yankee*, and made more cruises, but the Johnsons have not given up square sails because in 1976 they crossed the Atlantic in the barquentine *Regina Maris*.

Irving Johnson can be described as the real trail blazer of adventure voyages and found routes which have been followed by many other similar ventures. He went further than just making one highly-publicized voyage by really making a career of adventure voyaging. His books and magazine articles, particularly in the *National Geographical Magazine*, tell of the places the *Yankee* visited and the people who sailed with him, but reading between the lines one realizes that plain good honest seamanship and the ability to get along with people were the Johnson's main assets.

As we have seen, adventure voyaging became a recognizable feature in the years between the World Wars. Those early ocean wanderers had an advantage in that there was still a plentiful supply of full rigged sailing vessels, usually on the market cheaply because they were of no further use to the commercial world and were unsuitable for conventional yachts. But after World War II large sailing traders or fishermen were few and far between. Anyone wanting to make an ocean voyage in a traditional sailing ship after this had to first completely rerig and really create their own sailer. This is exactly what two Norwegian brothers did with the Baltic schooner *Regina*.

The *Regina* had been built by J Ring Andersen at Svendborg on the Danish Baltic island of Fyn in 1908. The Ring Andersen yard has always been one of the leading wood ship builders in Northern Europe, but this clipper-built cargo schooner was typical of dozens of other similar traders they built. Nor was her commercial career different from hundreds of other Baltic traders. By the time a bad fire in the engine room ended her trading days the vessel had been altered to a motor vessel. It was then that the Wilsons bought her and with some 60 tons of oak which they took back to Arendal in southern Norway, they completely rebuilt her as a barquentine *Regina Maris* – Queen of the Sea.

The Wilsons' family connection with the sea and sailing ships is old. The original family surname was Arnfinnson, but when John's and Sigfried's grandfather moved from Norway to Wales in 1876 he changed his name to Wilson. Later the family

The brigantine *Eye of the Wind* leaving Faversham Creek at the start of her world wandering. *Hugh Perks*

The brigantine *Eye of the Wind* rigged as the brig *Leonora* at Russell, Bay of Islands, New Zealand, for the making of the film 'Savage Islands'. *Clifford Hawkins*

returned to Norway and continued as sailors and ship owners.

Bred up in sail, the Wilson brothers dreamt that they too would command a sailing ship round Cape Horn. But they were a generation too late for this to be within the normal course of events. Norway found herself caught up in World War II, then in 1940 the brothers' father died. During the war two of his ships were sunk by the Nazis; the brothers survived though John suffered for two and a half years in a prisoner of war camp and Sigfried was held in a Nazi concentration camp until 1944 after being in the Norwegian Resistance.

After the war Sigfried continued in the army. John bought a ship and took command of her. In 1951 the brothers joined forces after John had acquired another ship and formed the Wilson Shipping Company with headquarters at Santiago, Chile. In 1956 the Company had two bulk ore carriers built in Japan and these ships were under Chilean charter.

In 1966 the Wilsons set out on their first voyage in *Regina Maris* round Cape Horn to Chile and later returned via New York to Norway. The purely technical difficulties of completely rebuilding and rerigging the *Regina Maris* were only some of the problems to be overcome before she went to sea. Because of her age and general background no North European country would accept her on their Shipping Register at that time. In the end she was accepted by Malta and became the *Regina Maris* of Valetta but she did not ever go near those Mediterranean islands. She spent the winter of 1968–9 at Arendal having her bottom sheathed with copper as a protection against the boring teredo worm which attacks wooden vessels in tropical waters. Her next voyage after this didn't put her in danger from the teredo worm as Radio Luxemburg chartered her for a publicity voyage along the French Coast to ports between Dunkirk and Bordeaux. After two months of this she crossed to Plymouth for a voyage to Australia to help celebrate the two hundredth anniversary of Captain Cook's landing in Australia. The *Regina Maris* was to sail out carrying dispatches from Norwegian and British dignitaries to the Australian High Commissioner and take part in a sailing ship rally at Sydney. At least this was the plan.

Captain Cook had started his voyage of discovery practically unnoticed when *Endeavour* warped out of Deptford Basin on 21 July 1768 and dropped anchor in the River Thames to take on guns and ammunition in Galleons Reach. Some two hundred years later the *Regina Maris* left Plymouth in a blaze of publicity to follow Cook's route. The Wilsons, as well as being first rate seamen, were fully aware of the value of keeping their barquentine within the public eye with good publicity but were not expecting the reason for their next attention received from the news media.

At about 9 am on the morning of 13 October the barquentine *Regina Maris* was dismasted. At the time she was in the Atlantic (lat 11deg 13mins N, long 26deg 44 mins W) making about five knots under all fore and aft and square sails with a moderate north-easterly breeze coming over the port quarter. It had been raining for an hour with ocasional lightning when suddenly a terrific gust accompanied by heavy rain hit the ship. She heeled and then with a tremendous crack the foremast collapsed over the starboard bow; at the same time the main and mizzen topmast snapped off and fell down into the shrouds. Very fortunately none of her crew were injured.

The wind then faded away leaving the barquentine wallowing in a long swell. The crew worked like slaves for the rest of the day cutting away wreckage and by late afternoon the foremast which had broken in four places and all the square sails, head sails, and staysails had sunk into the clear blue water. The work went on for the next two days, the topmasts were lowered to the deck and all the loose rigging sorted. It was discovered that the all-metal mizzen, which was also the outlet for the auxiliary exhaust, was fractured around the base.

The *Regina Maris* was over a week motoring slowly back to Gran Canaria. Many

The three-masted Baltic schooner *Golden Cachalot* in the Bay of Biscay outward bound to the Galapagos Islands in 1969. *Roger Jameson*

The foremast of the *Romance* shows how complex square sail gear is. However the square sails are very effective when running before the trade winds. *Captain A Kimberly*

people would have given up but the Wilsons took her back to Norway to be completely rerigged in the bitter northern winter. On February 13 she left Norway with basic fore and aft sails and only two square sails. She might have been icebound if the departure had been delayed any longer; as it was, two tugs were required to manoeuvre her through the first fifteen miles of the pack ice barrier.

On 17 February she was caught by a gale in the English Channel and put into Cowes

Roads, moving up to Southampton the following day for minor repairs which included a broken bobstay chain. After this the barquentine departed for Sydney, via Las Palmas and Cape Town for bunkering. After the dismasting some of the younger members of the crew had left and been replaced so that she was sailed with a crew of nineteen. The *Regina Maris* had been almost rerigged in only just over two months. The work was carried out at a small Kristiansand shipyard where some of the carpenters had worked a

Dugout canoes alongside the brigantine *Romance* at a Pacific atoll, c1976.
Captain A Kimberly

16-hour day in, at times, sub-zero temperatures. The new oregon pine lower foremast weighed 2½ tons, was 23ins in diameter at deck level and the total height was 110ft. This was slightly higher than before and although the sail area was about the same, the number of sails were increased to thirty-eight which still included the skysail and moonsail set above the royal. The mizzen mast was now wooden and was in fact the former main mast. On 9 March the *Regina Maris* reached Las Palmas having passed close to the island of Porto Santo (Madeira) on the night of 7 March. The passage from the English Channel was completed in light winds and the auxiliary was used extensively.

On June 6 the *Regina Maris* finally reached Sydney where she berthed at Circular Quay. The voyage from Capetown had taken forty-seven days which included a three-day stop at Albany, Western Australia, where she arrived to find the newspaper reporting her dismasted and presumed lost in the Indian Ocean! Including the time spent in ports the barquentine was ninety-nine days from England. The engine had been used in the doldrums and while on the passage from Cape Town two full gales were encountered. In one of these the wind probably reached force 10 and although the crew were working on the midships deck with water up to their thighs the only damage aloft was a split mizzen topsail and one broken stay.

From Australia she went to Tahiti and beat through the trade winds under fore-and-aft sails with the engine running. On 7 August a leak developed in the stern at a rate of about three tons of water an hour but this was controlled by the mechanised pumps. On 9 August she dropped anchor off Pitcairn Island and after paying a visit sailed for Cape Horn. Some of the crew became anxious about the leak because the pump was having to run continuously to keep the water in check. On 16 August a very heavy easterly gale blew up and kept the ship hove-to for three days. During this time the foretop and royal mast became loose and some of the crew became unwilling to continue the voyage. The Captain then decided to return via Peru where some of the young Norwegian crew left and then the *Regina Maris* continued to Panama to go through the canal and then return via Trinidad to Norway.

On the return trip the *Regina Maris* was carrying goodwill dispatches, hand written on parchment, from Australia which were going to be delivered to London. I remember late one November night in 1969 receiving a ship-to-shore phone message saying that *Regina Maris* would be passing under Tower Bridge at dawn the next morning and it seemed that there might be a chance of sailing on this now legendary ship – possibly even to Norway. Much of my night was taken up with just reaching London, but at dawn on Tower Bridge all that greeted me was wind and rain and great quantities of both. In fact the south-westerly gale sweeping over southern England caused the Master of *Regina Maris* to continue up the North Sea to Norway. Meanwhile on Tower Bridge it was, in spite of the roar of heavy traffic, remarkably lonely and I quietly wished that I had never heard of sailing ships.

The enormous expense of keeping a ship of this kind going was beginning to tell on the Wilsons and they sold her to Geg Cook of Palos Verdes Estates, Los Angeles who operated her as a holiday cruise ship in the Pacific. The first trip in this new role began in June 1971 when she sailed from Los Angeles with twenty-five passengers bound for Tahiti and was due to return via the Hawaiian Islands three months later. Paul Maskell

The cabin on the barque *Sea Cloud* when she was the yacht *Antama*. Millionaires used vessels like this as floating country homes and fitted them out in the same style.

had now taken over as Master. He came from the tiny coastal hamlet of Shingle Street in Suffolk and had originally seen the barquentine while he was a member of the Thames River Police. To start with he had followed the usual custom of just receiving his keep, no wages, but later on he had followed another Britisher Peter Wilson (no relation to the owners) as mate.

During the following summer *Regina Maris* was on a six-week cruise when she was caught in and almost overwhelmed by a hurricane. The passengers had paid for a voyage to Tahiti with intermediate stops at the Marquesas and Tuamotu Islands. About 1400 miles off Baja, California, the barquentine was hit by Hurricane Celesta. At the height of the storm the main engine and motor pumps broke down; she had plenty of searoom, but the violent motion of the huge seas was straining the wooden hull badly. With water rising in the hull both crew and passengers fought for thirty-six hours bailing manually. The U S Coast Guard responded to the distress call put out by the master by flying out and dropping five high speed pumps. However, since the weather was still bad and the *Regina Maris* was leaking badly, Captain Maskell arranged with the Indian freighter *Vishva Tirth* for a tow to Los Angeles.

Unfortunately the heavily-rigged barquentine did not prosper in the tourist adventure cruise game. On 5 May 1973 she arrived at Ensenada, Mexico, to finish her last Pacific charter. Here the ship was dry-docked and surveyed as part of the final arrangements for her sale to Brictec Finance of London. Paul Maskell had to end his six years with *Regina Maris* during which time he had kept with her throughout a dismasting, virtual mutinies and an assortment of near-misses.

For three years the *Regina Maris* was British owned and then in 1976 was bought by the Ocean Research & Education Society of Boston, Massachusetts. In the autumn of that year she had a major refit at Boston and then began a routine of going north to

55

Newfoundland and Greenland in the summer, primarily for the study of the whale, and renewing this study in the winter in the West Indies.

There are two sure ways of an adventure voyager receiving a wide coverage in news media. One is having some photographs of attractive young women in the rigging and the other is to get into some form of difficulty. The three-masted topsail schooner *New Endeavour* was owned by a group of Australians who had come to Europe with the express intention of buying a sailing ship and sailing her home on the same route as Captain Cook. She managed to attract attention to herself in both these ways when she sailed from Ramsgate in August 1965.

At that time coastal and inter-island trade in the Baltic was undergoing a steady decline and just about every harbour in Denmark and Southern Sweden had a few wooden traders laid up for sale. There were so many of them that they could be bought very cheaply. Although these Baltic traders were motor ships just about all of them had been built as sailers and had been steadily altered to power. The Australians had bought the ex-three-masted schooner *Dana*. She was really the ideal size for their purpose and her pedigree was right because she had been built of wood as the *Cito* by J Ring Andersen at Svendborg, Denmark in 1919 and this yard was noted for fine sailers. She was completely rerigged at Ramsgate on the south-east corner of England. When she sailed only the skipper, ex-British Royal Navy officer Gordon Keeble, and one of the other crew of twenty-one had any real sea experience. The rest of the crew had paid £400 for a six-month voyage to Australia. The difficulties at the start of the voyage were more embarrassing than disastrous. Not many miles out of Ramsgate the engine gears over-heated and for a time until this was sorted out the fast rescue boat from Walmer stood by.

The *New Endeavour* made her voyage safely to Australia and took up charter work from Mackay, North Queensland. This was a good base for passenger cruises along the Great Barrier Reef, Hayward and Whitsunday Islands during the Australian winter. During the summer she went south to Brisbane, Sydney and Melbourne to be clear of cyclones. The Sydney-based company which owned her got into financial difficulties in 1968 and the schooner was sold to Fauna Productions, a television film producing unit. They based her at Hayman Island, but luckily she was away from here when a cyclone flattened most of the buildings in 1970. However the schooner was attacked by the unseen enemy of the teredo worm who quietly took up residence in her wooden hull. In dry dock it was found that many of her underwater planks had literally been hollowed out by the boring worm and they had to be replaced. By this time *New Endeavour* had become a familiar sight on television screens in a number of series.

There is a special magic about sailing ships which causes people to drop their safe jobs ashore and sink all their savings into them. The voyage of the *New Endeavour* triggered off a whole series of sailing ship enterprises, one of which involved the 112ft Swedish motor ship *Eolus* which was brought to Ramsgate in 1970 and converted to a barquentine. Her voyage had so many set backs that it is best forgotten; however, before she finally sank in Malta in 1977, she almost rounded the world. Meanwhile the three-masted schooner *Aar* never even sailed from the River Tyne under the originally advertised voyage.

The Danish-built three-masted topsail schooner *Charlotte Rhodes*. This Dartmouth-based schooner made promotion voyages after her appearance in BBC Television's successful 'Onedin Line' series. In 1979 she was burnt out at Amsterdam.

A member of the *New Endeavour*'s crew who did manage to make the dream come true was the Londoner, Tony 'Tiger' Timbs who insisted on having a steel ship because when they had put the *New Endeavour* into a dry dock in Australia, the underwater planks had proved to be very badly eaten by teredo worms.

It was through this that I came in contact with him because by chance I had heard of the steel schooner *Merry* for sale at Gothenburg, Sweden. Timb's group bought the *Merry* in 1973 and brought her to Grimsby, an English fishing port on the River Humber, before moving her on to Faversham to complete her conversion to a brigantine.

It took a long time and a great deal of totally dedicated hard work to turn the former Swedish cargo trader *Merry* into the superb brigantine *Eye of the Wind*, but they did it without financial collapse or total mutiny. With the best will in the world, very few adventure voyagers have got the actual skill to rig out anything as complicated as a square-rigged brigantine. For this they enlisted the services of master rigger Walter Buchanan. Born in Liverpool, Wally first went to sea in steamers, but after World War

II he got a job as outside rigger in Cammell Lairds. Later he served a seven year apprenticeship as rigger at Harland & Wolff's Bootle yard. Here he was mate to an old Swedish master rigger who used to talk about how to rig the old sailing ships.

Wally Buchanan is now one of the few men who can not only splice wire rope, but also know how to make up the complex rigging needed to support the masts and control the sails. However, for a long time he wondered if he would ever get the chance to display his art. Then in 1965 he saw an advertisement for a rigger needed at Ramsgate for a schooner. That afternoon he was on the train down to join the schooner, the *New Endeavour*, which became the first of what Wally calls 'my ships'. The work on *New Endeavour* took four and a half months and he sailed to Lisbon on her first 'shake down' part of her voyage. Next came the barquentine *Eolus* which took five months. In between time he rerigged the Spanish ketch *Marques* into a polacca brigantine. The term 'polacca' means that the foremast is a single spar instead of three separate spars which make up the foremast of the usual northern European brigantine. Another job was rigging out the Baltic three-masted schooner *Gray* in five and a half weeks. He would also have rigged the *Aar* if that scheme had not fallen through. With this much experience it is hardly surprising that Wally Buchanan was recruited to do the wire standing rigging on the *Eye of the Wind*.

The mistakes and lessons learnt in the previous adventure voyages were considered when fitting out the *Eye of the Wind*. Firstly some of the owners had seen the *New Endeavour*'s teredo-eaten planks which made them determined to find a steel sailer for tropical waters. The choice of which rig to choose was confined to the traditional ones; no-one had any interest in the modern yacht sail plan because they would be totally out of character with this vessel. Making a long ocean voyage under sail is a romantic idea but the actual reality is much tougher. To fulfil this ideal the ship has to be a true 'trad' sailing ship. I first heard the word 'trad' in the early 1960s when trad jazz was a form of pop music. In ships it is sometimes used to embrace traditional, trading, training and tall ships, but there are some distinctions. Those vessels called traditional now are in fact the types and sail plans which were used between about 1890–1914, in fact the ones which were produced by centuries of trial and error. Not every ship with a rig based on the golden age of sail qualifies for the term 'trad'. For instance the British STA training schooners *Sir Winston Churchill* and *Malcolm Miller*, and the brig *Royalist* sailed by Sea Cadets, are superb sailing craft doing a very worthwhile job, but with their modern gear and hull shapes they are very different to the traditional ships like *Regina Maris* and *Eolus*.

For the venture to be really worthwhile the *Eye of the Wind* had to have a proper traditional rig. She could quite well have been rigged out again as a topsail schooner just as she had been when launched in 1911. For coastal and deep-water trading vessels in Northern Europe vessels of around 90ft in length with the square topsails on a schooner rig had proved to be highly practical. Certainly in the trade the 189 Thames ton *Gefion* had been worked by two men and two boys and then after being rigged out again as a very smart and handy topsail schooner she was sailed with a working crew of six across the Atlantic in the 1976 Tall Ships Races. This was a handy rig where the number of hands on deck were limited, but adventure voyages do not usually have a labour

Deck view of the
Charlotte Rhodes in the
Irish Sea, 1975. *Author*

shortage. Besides, a schooner, however good she is, is only a mere fore and aft rigged craft while a brigantine or barquentine which have square sails on the foremast are classified as real square riggers. This is a genuine attraction when recruiting both paying guests and working crews. However the final choice of brigantine for the *Eye of the Wind* was a practical consideration. She was to be used for mostly trade wind sailing and for continually running before the wind the square sails would unquestionably provide more driving power than the gaff sails of a schooner.

The *Eye of the Wind* left Faversham in September 1976 bound for Sydney. Many Australians have a love-hate relationship with their country's British origins and somehow sailing between the two countries takes on a particularly important significance. Captain James Cook set Australia's history in motion when he sailed out to survey the coast. In 1788, Britain having recovered from the loss of her most lucrative North American colonies dispatched some eleven ships from Portsmouth which sailed out to establish the first settlements at Botany Bay. For an Australian to sail from England is not just another adventure voyage, it is in fact retracing the lifeline of his country. The *Eye of the Wind* sailed with twenty-eight people on board; these included the Captain, Richard Grono, Tony Timbs, Lesley Ruber and Robert Partis as engineer. The guests had paid £1800 for an eight-month voyage to Australia.

After a week at Ramsgate the *Eye of the Wind* sailed on but met with such bad weather down the English Channel that she put into Brixham for shelter. When the weather moderated the brigantine put to sea again, but was hardly twenty-four hours out when she ran into really bad weather again. At one point the topgallant backstay carried away and the sails had to be hurriedly reduced to save the foremast from going over the side.

Madeira was the next stop and then on to Tenerife before crossing to Barbados. Some two months were spent cruising in the West Indies where they saw a 70ft trading schooner being built at Bequia. Christmas was spent at English Harbour, Antigua, and while at St Barts they were joined by the Windjammer Cruises' four-masted *Polynesia*, ex-Portuguese *Argus*.

By this time the brigantine rig had proved very effective for trade wind sailing. After leaving the Panama Canal she made for the Island del Coco where pirates are reputed to have buried their treasure, before visiting six of the Galapagos Islands where they were fascinated by the wildlife. From here the brigantine headed south, losing the trade winds at Lat 18° South, but headed on to Easter Island. This was the first Polynesian Island and they spent three enjoyable weeks there. Also at the anchorage was the American ferro-cement schooner *Good Ship Grace* which was being sailed by 'Christian Mariners' who intended spreading 'The Word' around the Pacific Islands. This ship had missed out the Galapagos Islands and finally on arrival at Easter Island most of the 'Mariners' had taken the advantage of the first scheduled jet back to the United States. Another visitor was Windjammer Cruises' *Yankee Trader* on her annual ten month world voyage.

Throughout the *Eye of the Wind*'s 1080 mile voyage from Easter Island to Pitcairn Island she was beset by calms and then head winds. For two days it blew force 9 with gusts of force 10. The ship handled well under double reefed gaff mainsail and shortened square sails. The motorship *Yankee Trader* hit the same patch of bad weather in the Southern Pacific and had one of her boats washed away. Pitcairn Island was finally sighted by the crew of *Eye of the Wind* at first light of their twenty-third day after leaving Easter Island. Pitcairn became the highlight of their voyage because from the very first moment when the boats came alongside and the islanders climbed over the bulwarks with baskets of fruit, the crew experienced warm hospitality and genuine kindness. Everyone on board spent at least one night ashore staying with a Pitcairn family. There was talk of the old days when the Islands' long boats propelled only by oars used to go off to meet the sailing ships whose names are now legendary. Ashore they saw cannons which had been recently brought up from the wreck of the famous British warship *Bounty*. One of the Island's modelmakers incorporates one of the *Bounty's* copper nails into each model.

They left Pitcairn with regret and the bows of the *Eye of the Wind* headed for Mangareva Island. The night before they were due to make their landfall a force 8 gale got up and since the entrance to the island's anchorage was very dangerous it was decided to miss this island and continue on to Papeeta on Tahiti. After this they spent another three months cruising through the Pacific islands to Sydney.

The *Eye of the Wind* spent seven weeks berthed at the Circular Quay, Sydney. There had been much nail-biting aboard before they arrived about whether passengers could be recruited for another voyage back to Europe to complete the round-the-world route. The brigantine's arrival out of the Pacific was well recorded in newspapers and on television. Her favourable progress up to that date meant that in fact she left Sydney in October, 1977 with twenty-nine people on board bound via the Barrier Reef, Indonesia, Singapore, Malaysia, the Indian Ocean, Red Sea and finally after Suez back to Plymouth. Here there was an offer of a charter for another world voyage for Operation Drake.

The *Eye of the Wind* was never intended to be just a once-only voyage ship; her owners wanted her to go on sailing as some form of charter ship. They seem to have overcome the continual threat of financial collapse which deals a final blow to so many adventure voyages. Finance is almost as great a problem as the never-ending perils of the sea. By using their engines most adventure voyages overcome the dangers but the sea does claim some.

The *Erawan*, a wooden Baltic schooner built in 1947, having some yards on the foremast laid claim to being a barquentine, but was smashed to pieces on the eastern Canadian Coast. Her last year seems to have been chequered with crew and financial problems, but in October 1976 after leaving the Great Lakes and heading out of St Lawrence River a gale in the Canso Strait put her ashore on the rocks off Cape Breton Islands. Her crew of eight were lucky to survive.

Then there was the loss of the 97ft barque *Endeavour II* which was driven ashore by a north-easterly gale at Parengarenga Harbour on the north east tip of New Zealand in February 1971. She was built as the *Monte Cristo* in British Columbia at Burrand Inlet, Vancouver, in 1965, but had been sold to an Australian who intended using her for charter work from Fiji but on passage from Brisbane intended calling at Auckland, New Zealand.

The barque's loss was the old, old story of a sailing ship getting caught on a lee shore. She had made good progress until reaching Lord Howe Island, but south of there the rigging became damaged. On reaching North Island, New Zealand, three attempts were made to get round Cape Karikari to reach the sheltered water of Houhora Harbour. The final effort was made under power, but when level with the Cape they ran out of fuel. She would probably have made it but a few days earlier she had wasted fuel searching fruitlessly for a boat in distress. Two anchors were let go but the ship dragged ashore and as she started to heel over the crew of fourteen abandoned her on two life rafts. The only casualty was the ship's cat Apollo. Within a few days the barque was nothing but a mass of planks strewn along a white sandy beach.

On the other side of the Northern Tasman Sea the topsail schooner *New Endeavour* also had trouble during this period of cyclones. She had been undertaking day charter cruises round Port Phillip Bay when she grounded on an unmarked reef and damaged her keel by grinding on the rocks. For repair it was decided to go north along the Australian East Coast to a dry dock at Ballina, New South Wales. In the strong wind she delighted her crew on the passage by making seven knots under lower topsail and storm jib. They arrived at Ballina early and had to anchor in nearby Byron Bay and wait, but during this time a heavy swell began to get up and they learnt that a cyclone was approaching. To have remained at anchor would have meant that the *New Endeavour* was in danger of being swamped and swept ashore. With the wind increasing to force 9, around 40 knots speed, and the schooner now plunging wildly they had a desperate job recovering the anchor. Luckily for them the eye of the cyclone passed to the north and *New Endeavour* managed to get safely to the shelter of Brisbane.

Charter work in Port Phillip Bay from Melbourne was later started by the brigantine *Golden Plover*. Her steel hull was originally the steamer *Plover*, built in 1910, but after being completely gutted by fire in 1968 she was excellently transformed into a little square rigger. She proved herself by making a voyage to Europe, through the Suez Canal in 1977.

Like many of the small square riggers she was actually given a rig from the mid-Victorian period. This means only crossing three yards on the foremast and setting a course, single topsail and a single topgallant sail above. Between the masts are set three staysails, the main staysail, nock staysail and topmast staysail. The term 'nock' is an old one meaning a four-sided fore-and-aft sail. Although the rig does look rather 'old fashioned' compared to the four masted barques of the 1890s and the modern square-rigged training ships, these modern brigantines tend to carry much larger staysails than the older trading vessels. Certainly the Canadian Great Lakes training brigantines *St Lawrence II*, *Pathfinder* and *Playfair* can stow up their square sails and beat to windward under fore-and-aft sails like a schooner. Even the modern training brig *Royalist* appears to do the same.

The 86ft ex-Danish jagt-built *Romance* looks 'old fashioned' for the very reason that she was bought by an American film company and converted into an 1820s-style brigantine for the film 'Hawaii'. After this in March 1966 Captain Arthur Kimberly bought her. The American Captain Kimberly had been at sea for twenty-five years starting in the four-masted barque *Abraham Rydberg* and then in tankers. He has the rare distinction of holding papers as a master in sail. The *Romance* is based at St Thomas in the US Virgin Islands for charter. This makes practical sense because the passengers can fly down from the States and then spend a pleasant eight days cruising round the islands.

Captain Arthur Kimberly's committal to sail is certainly not just another project to make money from tourists. He runs a cadet-training scheme and every so often leaves the Caribbean to make a long voyage. The longest of these has been a twenty-month round-the-world voyage beginning in October 1975. After leaving St Thomas the *Romance* with the help of the trade winds covered the first thousand miles to Panama in six days four hours, and after entering the Pacific began to island-hop across that great ocean.

Finding an abandoned sailing ship's hull has a special sensation which only a true devotee to sail can really understand. Certainly Captain Kimberly knew just what that feeling meant when he visited the hulk of the 2900-ton *County of Roxburgh* on a lonely Pacific island while continuing his round-the-world voyage. While in the Marquesas Islands Captain Kimberly had read through his thirty-year collection of *Sea Breezes* magazines and noted that the four-masted full rigged ship *County of Roxburgh* had been wrecked in the Tuamotus Archipelago which was the next group of islands ahead.

The ship was built by Barclay, Curle in 1886 for R & J Craig who owned a total of twelve four-masted full rigged ships. The *County of Roxburgh* was in the India-Scotland jute trade until going into general tramping in the Pacific. In 1905 she had left Caldera, bound across the Pacific in ballast when a furious hurricane overtook the ship and drove her ashore on Takaroa.

On 19 January 1976 the brigantine *Romance* arrived at Takaroa and there, still on the beach, was the *County of Roxburgh*. On the Island they met Captain Omer Darr, the veteran South Sea schooner master, who told them that some of the ship's masts had still been standing in 1947. These have now fallen down but the bowsprit was still complete. Very little of the removable equipment remained although the four anchors were still there. The port bower (anchor) was actually still hooked on to the forecastle rail. More incredible, after some seventy years of tropical sun, it was possible to trace some of the original colour scheme. Also enough of the deck fittings remained for Captain Kimberly to work out what her deck layout had been.

The first real drama that occurred with *Romance* was at Singapore when during a sudden squall at 3am a derelict steamer swung into her with the result that the topgallant backstay was unhooked and the mast snapped. Most of the expense-sharing crew (everyone stands watch on *Romance*) had flown to Bangkok, but the skipper, mate Dan Moreland, Jim Brinks and entire remaining crew worked like demons to send down sails, rigging, yards and broken topgallant mast and rerig everything within a week so that the brigantine sailed again on time.

At sea again the *Romance* was sailing in company with Very Large Crude Carriers and after these VLCC superships she was amongst oil rigs which made the night sky a blazing inferno. In the Bangka Straits she came upon a disabled wooden steamer trying to make sail with hatch covers. Her young Indonesian crew had been without food for three days and were very glad of the stores given by *Romance*. After going through the Sunda Straits they began a wild wet slog to windward across the Indian Ocean to reach

The Dutch schooner *Johanna Lucretia* was built as a wooden Belgian motor fishing vessel in 1945. With the supply of ex-sailing ship hulls suitable for conversion back to sail drying up, the alternative is to convert any hull with reasonably fine lines. *Author*

the Cocos Keeling Islands. Six days later they let their heavy anchor go in five fathoms off Direction Island, Cocos Keeling. This tiny group of islands has been the private kingdom of six generations of the John Clunes Ross family and their Malay plantation workers. The present JCR insists on complete privacy on Home Island, but allows visitors on Direction Island. After the crowded Orient the *Romance*'s people found empty sandy beaches and warm lagoons a welcome change.

This was just the first of the Indian Ocean Islands visited on their way to the Seychelles and then down to South Africa. The 800-mile passage from Durban to Cape Town included sailing in the stormy waters off the Cape of Good Hope. The *Romance* was soon to be fighting the largest seas she had encountered in a decade of sailing. New Years Day 1977 found the *Romance* hove-to in a full gale under double sheeted mainstaysail and three oil bags out. This is an old seafaring practice; the oil forms a film over the surface and tends to prevent the crests of the sea from breaking with such fury. The *Romance* slid harmlessly over a continual roaring series of grey-green mountains without coming to any harm. Nearing Cape Town there was another gale which she rode under bare poles at night, but was still making 4 knots and at one stage it looked as if she was going to be blown past Cape Town. At dawn, there was Table Mountain and a low fog bank obscuring the harbour, making an unforgetable sight as the little wooden brigantine entered to be given a warm welcome. In their honour a Cape Horner's Party was given and seventeen ex-Cape Horn seamen who had served in twelve ships turned up. South Africa had run the four-masted barque *Lawhill* through World War II and the memories of those days lived on.

After this visit *Romance* set out on her last ocean crossing of this voyage. From Cape Town to Rio de Janiero she crossed 3890 beautiful sparkling blue miles of the lonely South Atlantic in thirty six days. She had, that most lovely of things to a sailing ship, a fair wind. For twenty-six continuous days the stuns'ls (extra sails on the outside of the normal square sails) were kept set. The stuns'ls were used by the famous clipper ships, but not by the later four-masted barques such as *Lawhill* and *Abraham Rydberg*. The only other contemporary square rigger to have them was *Regina Maris*. It is a long time since any ship has run for such a long period with stuns'ls set and it may not happen again for many years because none of the large training ships bother with stuns'ls. Most of them simply start their engines when the wind drops because they run to schedule and have their berths and official engagements arranged ahead.

For the last part of the voyage the *Romance* had to beat her way 1700 miles north against the wind and the strong Brazilian current to get round the fat bulge of South America. It took twenty-one days to raise the island of Fernando de Noronha. After this there was only 2000 miles back to St Thomas but they felt they were nearly home. Finally on April 29 after sailing from Trinidad the *Romance* crossed her outward bound track and the circumnavigation was over.

When it was all over the facts were added up. She had sailed 33,369 nautical miles at an average speed of 4.2 knots. (The brigantine *Eye of the Wind* reckoned to have averaged about 5 knots from England to Australia.) Her best noon to noon day's run was 174 nautical miles while the shortest day's run was 54 nautical miles. Her best average passage speed was Cape Town to Rio de Janiero at 4.4 knots. The masters of large square riggers claim that stuns'ls were of no use but they certainly helped *Romance*; perhaps they work better on smaller vessels.

In 1982 the British brig *Ciudad de Inca*, again a ship about the size of *Romance*, tried out stuns'ls and her master, Mark Litchfield, was very pleased with the extra speed they produced.

In the 1970s there was an almost continual stream of former Baltic traders leaving Denmark and south Sweden on voyages to the West Indies and the Pacific. By 1980 most of the former traders had been sold, but yards such as Ring Andersen's at Svendborg and Jacobsens Plads across the Sound at Troense have had continual work rebuilding and rigging out sailing vessels. This is just one area of Denmark and other yards in the north have been just as busy. Most of the schooners have been sold to American and German owners, while the Danes have mostly only been able to keep the smaller traders or former fishing craft.

Most of these Baltic traders never catch public attention unless they get into serious trouble, as the 89ft three-masted topsail schooner *Activ* did when she was lost with everyone on board in the North Sea in February, 1983. The *Activ* was in very good order when she left Ramsgate with eight young people aboard, all anxious to make a return passage to Denmark. But it appears that they seriously underestimated the force of a winter's gale in the North Sea. The day after she sailed, the wind reached hurricane force and the *Activ* radioed from 22 miles north-west of Texel, the Netherlands, that she was making water. Shortly afterwards she radioed that she had a 40 degree list and that was the end of the schooner and her crew, in spite of heroic efforts made by the Netherlands Navy to make a rescue.

The *Activ*'s tragic loss lead to a tightening up of regulations regarding Danish sailing vessels, and the schooner's owners, the Twind School of Nyborg, a liberal cooperative attempting to run a society on absolute equality, began to sell its fleet of sail trainers. Another Baltic training scheme run on liberal lines is the ketch *Fri*. In 1974 she sailed from Wellington, New Zealand, to hit the world headlines when she sailed into French nuclear testing grounds as an active protest against nuclear explosions. The *Fri* of Aalborg was built in Denmark in 1912 and is a typical jagt-built galease. The round bow and transom stern gave her plenty of buoyancy. In 1969 she arrived at Leith from Copenhagen with a Danish crew to load cases of Drambuie whisky for New York. She was already under the American flag and this voyage appears to have been a form of advertisement. Quite a number of sailing ships manage to finance themselves on sales promotion trips to that there was nothing new in this.

The *Fri* of San Francisco, owned by American David Moody, arrived at Wellington in July 1974 with the mission of protesting against the forthcoming French nuclear tests and continued on to make a two year nuclear protest voyage. The 'peace boat' *Fri* collected protest postcards written by New Zealanders and these were to be given to the Heads of States at the countries she visited. She had been fitted out at Tauranga in New Zealand's North Island for a long stay at sea and the first form of protest was sailed into the French area so as to make it impossible to explode their device. It was brave and courageous act to take because the French could have chosen to ignore them and the *Fri* and crew would have been wiped from the face of the world in a second. This would of course have earned the French a great deal of bad publicity, but world public opinion has a surprisingly short memory while those protesting on the *Fri* would have been gone for ever.

The French Navy on the other hand had received orders to prevent the ketch from making any form of public protest. They forcibly removed the *Fri* from the area by towing her to Tahiti. The *Fri* sailed on to deliver messages of peace all over the world. I believe she entered Russian waters at Vladivostok, but received a very cool reception and was also refused entry into Chinese communist ports. It seems naive to think that one sixty-three year old Baltic trading ketch could change the course of world opinion but surely no small sailer ever carried a more important message. The existance of the terrifying destructive nuclear weapons means that unless a way is found for mankind to live together in peace, we could all be destroyed in some disastrous future war.

The former Danish galease (trading ketch) *Fri* sailing from Wellington, New Zealand bound for the French nuclear bomb testing area in the Pacific in an attempt to stop a nuclear explosion, 1974. *V H Young*

CHAPTER 4

Working Sail

The cruel unrelenting sea is a common enemy to all ships, but each ship also has to survive within the economic and social framework of the port which sent her to sea. The most extreme examples of this are in the Third World. For instance the port of Mombasa on the east coast of Africa is served by modern freighters, but in the old town the dhows handle the local trade in a truly medieval way with everything being done by hand labour. Off Mombasa, when freighters pass a dhow, they are a thousand years apart in social development.

Working sailing craft exist in economic pockets dotted all over the world, but in a century of relentless technical progress these pockets can be wound up overnight. In Britain, hundreds of schooners and ketches were built for general coastal trades, but in the economic slump of the 1920s most of this trade was taken by diesel vessels, particularly by the Dutch motor coasters. However around the Bristol Channel purely local conditions created an economic pocket in which sailing coasters, fitted with low powered engines, survived for another thirty years.

The Bristol Channel, which leads into the River Severn, cuts a great natural barrier between the coalfields of South Wales and the Forest of Dean, and the small towns and villages in Devon and Cornwall. The railway and road transport around the Bristol Channel was a long and expensive business so the schooners and ketches, with small consignments of coal, could just about earn a living.

In rural north Devon there was a lack of employment so men were glad to go to sea. The bleak little town of Appledore on the low peninsular between the sea and the River Torridge and the more rural village of Braunton continued their nineteenth century tradition of operating skipper-owned schooners and ketches. Yet the returns from coal and animal food stuff cargoes from the ports of South Wales were not high enough for shareholders to amass enough capital to buy new ships. There was a flurry of rebuilding in the boom conditions just after World War II, but from the late 1920s this fleet of sailing traders had been doomed.

It can take long, back-breaking hours of pumping to keep an aging wooden hull afloat, and one by one the north Devon men gave up the struggle and abandoned their vessels on the mud above Appledore. The final blow came in the late 1950s when oil started to replace coal, making the mainstay of the North Devon trade vanish. The last two to give up were the ketch *Irene* and Captain Tom Jewell's schooner *Kathleen & May* which were laid up for sale at Appledore in 1960. The Braunton-owned steel schooner

Result actually went on in general trade until her captain Peter Welch died in 1967, but she had been converted to a motor vessel.

Once a tradition is completely broken it is very hard to start again. When the Hudson's Bay Company wanted a replica built of their first ship, the seventeenth century square-rigged ketch *Nonsuch*, it was suggested that because of Appledore's connection with sail, it should be built there. However even in 1969 when Hinks yard launched the *Nonsuch* there were very few people locally with much interest in sailing such a vessel. Hinks went on to build a number of wooden replicas.

In 1983 the only reminder of Appledore's past was in a neat little museum overlooking the Torridge and the only vessel left in the river was the little ketch *Maria* on the mud opposite Bideford. Unfortunately, the north Devon vessels dropped out of trade just before the great revival of interest in such craft in the early 1960s.

To understand sailing vessels one must understand the trades and fisheries that each particular type of vessel was evolved for. It is worth looking at a few of these occupations in detail and studying the very few craft which have worked under sail in the western world in more recent times.

Some of the most seaworthy and hard driving fishing craft were the Gloucester schooners which were used in North America from New York right up to the Canadian province of Newfoundland. It was the rich fishing grounds in this part of the Atlantic which first attracted Europeans in large numbers to North America. By the early 1500s the French, Portuguese, Spanish and British fishermen were coming annually to New England and Labrador. Rivalry between the fishermen was intense and details of the fishery were kept secret. The English and the French established shore bases and a power struggle developed for control of the whole continent.

Early fishing on the banks off the north American coast was done with handlines from the boats. In the mid-twentieth century the French-speaking Canadians of Quebec still used this method from little clinker Gaspé schooners. However, in the New England States in the 1850s the practice grew of carrying open dories on the decks of the schooners which were launched each day and the men went out fishing with long handline 'trawls'. The New England, Nova Scotia and Newfoundland schooners seem to have carried 'double banked' (two-man dories) while the French and Portuguese had

A British topsail schooner in about 1900 rounding the Needles on the Isle of Wight. She appears to be sailing light between cargoes.

one-man dories. The schooners did not usually anchor, but remained drifting on the tide with the dories spread out around them for about a mile. It was obviously a dangerous method of fishing. Fog or sudden wind changes resulted in the loss of many dorymen each year. To make it worse the Grand Banks lay on passenger routes between Europe and America and schooners and dories were often run down by express liners ploughing through the fleets at speed to keep up with their timetables.

At the Nova Scotian fishing port of Lunenburg flat-bottomed dories were first carried on the cod schooners in about 1870. However many fishermen in Nova Scotia tried to get the dory trawl method banned. They were unsuccessful, for within a decade it was in general use. This new method led to greater expansion in Nova Scotia's offshore fishing fleet. At Lunenburg two companies on the waterfront began to build up a thriving trade exporting dried salted cod to the West Indies and mackerel to the United States. These merchants also gave credit to fishermen to build and equip new schooners so that Lunenburg, although only a small remote out-port, began to develop a thriving fishing fleet.

By 1888 Lunenburg County had 193 'salt bankers' (fishing schooners) employing 4842 men and boys. The wealth these produced over the following decades can still be seen in the heavily-decorated wooden houses in the attractive little town of Lunenburg. However the town always suffered a manpower shortage as there was a continual drift of men down to New England.

At Lunenburg in 1980 I was told by eighty-year-old Paul H Mosher that dory fishing had been such a hard life that the fishermen considered it virtually slavery. Lunenburg had been originally settled by German protestants in 1753 and Paul Mosher, like most Lunenburgers of his generation, still spoke in the old dialect which sounds like Westcountry English spoken with a German accent. He was one of a family of twelve; his father had been a fisherman and had owned sixty-four shares in schooners. These sixty-four shares represented one 'whole vessel', but Mosher senior had kept his shares in separate schooners to spread the risk.

Lunenburgers liked to name their schooners after their women folk, usually after the wife or daughter of the largest shareholder. Paul Mosher had started at sixteen as a dory fisherman. He sailed in the schooners *Pauline Mosher* and *Sylvia Mosher* and went down to

The Canadian fishing schooner *Dorothy M Smart* laid up at Digby, Nova Scotia. *Nova Scotia Museum*

the West Indies in the *Edith Newhall* to spend the winter trading in the islands. Other schooners spent the winter laid up at anchor in the little bay in front of the town. In the summer men from miles around left their farms and went out on to the banks in the schooners. It was a dismal working life being all day out on the open ocean tending the trawls. If their day's catch was good then they spent half the night salting the fish down in the hold. If the weather was reasonable the next day, at sunrise the dories were lowered again and away they went because every moment of good weather had to be used.

Only once did Paul Mosher become separated from his schooner, when the fog came down rapidly. For a long time they could hear her gun firing as a signal, but he still could not find her. At around midnight the fog lifted and they could see a schooner's riding light about five miles away. The other man in the dory said that it might not be their schooner, but Paul Mosher said they had better start rowing as any vessel was better than none. Luckily it was theirs.

Paul's elder brother was the Captain and he refused to fish on a Sunday. Not for religious reasons, but because usually the men were nearly exhausted. Captain Mosher used to say 'This life is hard enough, if we can't get enough fish in six days then we will not come to this place at all'.

Three of Mosher's brothers were schooner captains and two of these were lost with their vessels. One of them had wanted to come ashore to finish building his house and suggested that Paul went as Captain on the next trip. But the last time this brother was seen was when another Lunenburg Captain went aboard his vessel and was told that they were loaded but were going to stay another day so that the men could catch some fish for themselves. No trace of the schooner or her crew were ever seen again and it was believed that she was one of the many hundreds of ships driven ashore on Sable Island.

The knockabout (no bowsprit) fishing schooner *Athena*, built in Maine in 1910. She foundered at sea in 1921. *Peter Dawson*

The loss of these schooners was a very heavy blow to a small community like Lunenburg. The figures given in 1926 were that fifty men were lost in two schooners while in the following year a further eighty men were lost in four schooners. For a fishing town there was nothing new in their men being taken by the sea. In the old days the wives and family of drowned fishermen had to suffer complete poverty alongside their grief, but by the 1920s the Canadian law said that families had to be compensated. This was a very correct and humane step, but it did throw further financial strain on the remaining schooners which were trying hard to survive the Great Depression. The end result was that Lunenburg's schooner numbers dropped from seventy-two in 1929 right down to twenty-six in just three years.

The salt bank schooners had evolved in Massachusetts for the schooner owners at Gloucester. The Gloucester clipper schooners of 1870–1900 were mainly built for speed, but so many were lost that they tried to make them more seaworthy. Since so many men were washed off the bowsprit while stowing sails they did away with them by extending the bow a long way forward. The result was the spoon-bowed knockabout schooners. The Americans lost interest in these schooners and went over to powered vessels, but Canadians continued to develop the type into motor schooners.

The first knockabout schooners built at Lunenburg was the *General Haig* from Smith & Rhuland yard at the end of the little waterfront, in 1918. The first full-powered knockabout Lunenburg type schooner appeared in about 1930. They used engines on passage to the banks, but while fishing they hove to under sail. The last of the Lunenburg sail-using schooners was the *Theresa E Connor* which is preserved in the town. This later type of vessel was fishing both in summer and winter.

It would be impossible to discuss Lunenburg without mentioning the *Bluenose* which was the most famous of the North American schooners ever built. Fishermen in New England and Nova Scotia watched the America's Cup yacht race with tremendous

At Lunenburg the dory fisherman Paul Mosher with the schooner *Theresa E Connor* in the background. This schooner, now a museum ship, was one of the motor schooners which operated summer and winter between 1934–63. They used to motor sail on passage and then hove-to under sail while the dories went out longlining. *Author*

professional interest and finally decided to hold their own International Fishermen's trophy. What started as a bit of sport for the cod fishermen quickly developed into a highly publicised battle between the United States and Canada. Actually, so many men had left the Maritime Provinces to go and work from New England ports that it was almost a Nova Scotian vessel versus Nova Scotian men who had gone to New England.

In order to produce a winner for this Trophy a group of Lunenburg men asked the Halifax designer William Roue to design a schooner. The result was the *Bluenose*, but

The Newfoundland motor schooner *Norma & Gladys* with dories on deck and the huge wooden stock anchor.

as she took shape on Smith & Rhuland's slipway in 1921 they decided to alter the shape of her bow. Nova Scotians have been trying to imitate that bow ever since, but at the time Roue was furious at the departure from his plans and refused to have his name linked with the schooner. He soon changed his attitude when *Bluenose* proved to be an almost unbeatable winner.

When the Chebucto Fishing Company asked Roue to design a schooner to beat *Bluenose*, he had her built at Shelburne, further down the southern shore, so that his

Dory on the deck of the Newfoundland motor schooner *Shirley Blanche*. *Author*

design would not be altered. The result was the beautiful *Haligonian*, but she was a disappointment. When the *Haligonian* was sailed hard her fine bow became buried in the sea while the high bow of the *Bluenose* lifted her above the water. Later the Royal Canadian Navy had the training ship *Venture* built from the original *Bluenose* plans but she does not appear to have given an outstanding performance.

The original *Bluenose* was wrecked in 1946 and in 1963 *Bluenose II* was built from the same plans for publicity cruises. Immediately there were arguments as to whether she was as fast as the legendary *Bluenose* of 1921. The truth will never be known, but *Bluenose II* is credited with sailing at 18 knots in ideal conditions. By 1966 her fastest passage was the 387.5 miles from Boston Harbour to Halifax Harbour at an average speed of 10 knots. This included the time spent in each harbour, so she must be a fast schooner.

These schooners needed speed to sail the long distances to the fishing grounds and also when they took freights of dried cod to the West Indies and Europe. The Newfoundlanders never developed their own schooners for long passages, but relied on the British and Danish schooners and ketches to come across for the dried salted 'stockfish' cod. The Newfoundland schooners were much plainer than those of Nova Scotia, but they went on working far longer.

On the Island of Newfoundland and the coast of Labrador, most of the people live in tiny settlements clinging to the rocky coast. They developed the beamy diesel schooners for this coastal trade which set a knockabout (no bowsprit) rig of jib, forestaysail, gaff foresail and triangular trysail on the after mainmast. These schooners called in at the tiny fishing settlements with gasoline, machinery, salt and every conceivable imported goods and loaded dry fish out. Fishing gradually took second place. The 92ft schooner *Norma & Gladys*, built by four fishermen at Trinity Bay in 1945 only went one season dory fishing and then went freighting. The 110ft *Philip E Lake* also only went to the Grand Banks once after being built in 1948 and then also switched to freighting.

In the 1960s there was a great road building programme throughout eastern Canada and trucks began to take over haulage work in Newfoundland. By the 1970s most of the remaining Newfoundland schooners were up for sale in a land which had little use for yachts. Many of these were sold to the States such as the case of the 101ft *Shirley Blanche*, built at Burin in 1949. While fishing she had carried ten two-man dories which went out for fish while the Captain, mate, engineer and cook worked the schooner. When I went aboard the *Shirley Blanche* at Shelburne, Nova Scotia, in 1980 she was supposed to be on her way to the West Coast, but her voyage south had been a catalogue of disasters. Many former working craft have fallen into the hands of people who have lacked resources or the ability to look after them. A year later the *Shirley Blanche* had made it to the States with more disasters in the Delaware and Chesapeake Bays. The last information was that in 1983 this schooner had sunk at Hampton, Virginia. She deserved a better end.

The only place in North America where sailing vessels still work is in Chesapeake Bay where on the eastern Maryland shore it is forbidden for powercraft to dredge oysters. In 1976 I travelled to this part of the United States to seek for this working fleet. Finding the fleet took quite a while as the Chesapeake is a wide estuary extending inland from the Atlantic for 195 miles, but eventually I located them working from Tilghman Island. Next morning before dawn I sailed on the skipjack *E C Collier* for a day's dredging in the Choptank River. As the first streaks of dawn appeared on the horizon it was possible to pick out the white sails of the skipjacks. None were fitted with engines, but some were being pushed by their powered 'yawl' boats. In the cold dawn it gradually became possible to count nineteen skipjacks and I was fascinated to learn more about these remarkable craft and the background to their continued existence.

Chesapeake Bay is really one of the world's largest estuaries, in fact it is more like an inland sea. The State of Virginia covers the lower end and does not have the 'no power' rule. In Maryland the rural eastern shore of Chesapeake Bay is a mass of small islands and river mouths cutting into the low country. The Choptank river is the largest of these and the oysters thrive in its shallow waters.

Since the area was first settled by Europeans in the 1600s the gathering of seafoods and waterfowling had been a major feature of life for the small and until quite recently remote communities on the eastern shore. It is estimated that in 1898, 2247 skipjacks, schooners, sloops and bugeyes were licenced to dredge under sail in Chesapeake Bay and obviously even then they were exhausting the natural supply of

oysters. Most of the laws regulating shell fishing are aimed at limiting the numbers taken. Maryland only allows oysters to be harvested between November 1 and March 3 and can only be dredged between sunrise and sunset. Oysters can only be marketed until an hour after sunset. Most of the oysters are now taken by two-man tongers. From these power boats long drop tongs are used to scoop up oysters by hand while the sailing skipjacks use large dredges. The shallower oyster bars are reserved

The Chesapeake Bay skipjack *Lady Katie* with one reef down, dredging oysters in the Choptank River, 1976. *Author*

Sorting oysters on the skipjack *E C Collier* with the *Lady Katie* ahead. *Author*

The skipjack *Martha Lewis* being pushed by her yawl into Tilghman, Maryland, USA. The power tongers are in the dock behind. *Author*

for the tongers; however, many people working on the water would like to see regulations relaxed and some easier form of oyster harvesting adopted. In the fall of 1976 there were only twenty-seven skipjacks left working and everyone I spoke to believed that sail would die out quite quickly.

That November morning the skipjacks spread out over the Choptank, every Captain going where he believed the oysters would be the thickest. Aft at the wheel of the *E C Collier* Captain John Larrimore was steering for a spot he guardedly referred to as 'up the river'. Back at 5.30am when boarding for the day's dredging, Captain John and his cousin Captain Stanley Larrimore of the *Lady Katie* had had a quiet discussion about the weather and where the wind made it most suitable for dredging. The fresh breeze and the power yawl hurried the *E C Collier* over the eleven miles to the oyster bar near the Choptank light. While Captain John Larrimore stayed at the wheel the other men went down into the aft cabin. Below from his place beside the bottle gas stove Peewee, who acted as cook, handed out ample helpings of breakfast which was washed down with good strong coffee. It was too early for much conversation, just a few remarks in Southern drawl about 'peanut butter' Jimmy Carter coming out the winner in the Presidential Election results given out the previous night.

Apart from Captain John, the only other white aboard was his grandson Johnny Cummings, who really worked a tonger, but was on board to learn sail 'drudging' to eventually take over. He and Captain John had spent the previous summer raising the aft deck and building a higher cabin. But sixty-seven year old Captain John showed no signs of wanting to give up and said that he would go on dredging 'just as long as he could crawl aboard and had the strength to stand at the wheel'.

On the skipjacks they followed the normal practice of small working craft in that the master stood at the wheel all the time. When dredging this could mean for all the winter daylight hours, but in the summer they went laying oyster shells and the

76

The Delaware Bay oyster schooner *Richard Robbins Sr* being rebuilt at Rockland, Maine, 1976. *Author*

Captain could be at the wheel from 4am until 9pm. The crew also said that shovelling shells was harder work than dredging.

Once the Choptank light had been reached the yawl was hauled up into the stern davits and dredging under sail began. The first 'lick' with the dredges was to find the thickest oysters. Once the spot was found, a buoy was put down and the rest of the day was spent dredging around it. The routine was simple but effective. A large dredge was worked from each side, each looked after by a team of three. When Captain John gave the order, actually a mere cough, the dredges were pushed over and the full length of a wire rope. To recover them, usually after about three minutes, the Captain pulled the cord which tripped the motor-driven power winders into action which then hauled the full dredges back on to the deck. Here the oysters were tipped out and sorted at speed. Captain John put the skipjack about for another reach and down went the dredges again.

Once the wind freshened so that the jib had to be reefed, but normally no one had time to touch the sails and the skipjack literally had to sail herself. It was solely for oyster dredging in these shallow but quite sheltered waters that skipjacks were first evolved back in the 1890s. The *E C Collier* is 55ft long, 18ft beam and 5ft draught, but dropping the all-important centreboard adds an extra 5ft to her draught. She is one of the largest skipjacks, but the largest is said to have been the 60ft *Robert L Webster* built in 1915. The hard chine hull design meant that the skipjacks were cheap to build and fast to sail, making up to twelve knots in the right conditions but they were never sea boats. Of course Captain John had had a lifetime's experience to draw on so was able to turn his skipjack about all day over the bar, often within a few feet of the *Lady Katie* who was dredging the same spot. However the *E C Collier* was the handiest sailing working craft that I have been aboard.

At Deal Island I had spoken to men who had dredged in schooners until 1939, but these and other types of Chesapeake Bay oyster boats had been replaced by the easy to handle skipjacks. An old type had been the 'bugeye', double ended, centreboard craft with sharp headed sail and ketch rig. The hull had developed from the original log canoe. Once too there had been round bottomed craft rigged as topmast sloops. The skipjack-rigged *Rebecca T Ruark* which came down from Cambridge to dredge in the lower Choptank that morning started off as one of these and the only other round bottomed skipjack left was the *Susan Mae*. However the last real working gaff headed sloop had been the *J T Leonard*, built 1881, which was given to the Chesapeake Bay Maritime Museum at St Michaels for preservation. In March 1976 the museum broke her up with a bulldozer. However the museum was in the process of completely rebuilding the 53ft log bottom bugeye *Edna E Lockwood* built at Tilghman's in 1889.

To the crew of *E C Collier* they were more concerned with making a good wage than historic boat preservation. At about 11am they stopped work for a hurried meal prepared by Peewee in between helping to sort oysters. By early afternoon the four piles of oysters began to look impressively large and it was obvious that the daily limit of 150 bushels would soon be reached. The *Lady Katie* sailed close under the stern and Captain Stanley said he had reached his limit and was off home. A few more licks and Captain John reckoned that he could tell that he had reached the limit.

With the strong breeze the *E C Collier*'s long clipper bow was pointed back towards Tilghman Island. Her beamy hull seemed little affected by the considerable extra weight on deck although there have been cases of loaded skipjacks capsizing in sudden squalls. Everyone was pleased that the day's oyster limit had been reached. The skipjack earnings were split three ways, the first third to the boat, then expenses and finally the remainder was divided equally amongst the seven men aboard. The oystermen on the skipjacks were earning above average for a labouring man in this part of the United States although in the winter they lost time through gales and ice.

There was no financial advantage in being home first; the oysters were all sold at more or less standard prices on the wharf and mostly taken away in waiting trucks. Before World War I 'buying' schooners used to sail round the Bay. After this the buyers went round in power boats and purchased the oysters afloat from the dredgers and tongers. However this meant that the oysters all had to be handled twice and in the 1950s it became the custom to sell oysters to the merchants on shore.

The sight of two skipjacks heading for home caused a group which had been dredging on the opposite shore to sail over and try to find our good spot. The leader was *H M Krentz* which was one of the Deal Island skipjacks. These work in the upper Bay from the beginning of the season until Christmas; they of course go into harbour every night, but the crews live aboard. After the Chesapeake Bay Appreciation Day Race at Sandy Point they had intended to land their oysters there. As Sandy Point is within a State Park where no commercial activities are permitted the Rangers had forbidden them to unload there so that the Deal Island skipjacks had moved across to Tilghman Island.

Racing working sailing boats in the Eastern United States was largely stimulated by the famous America Cup Race between yachts. This led to the great International Fisherman's Cup Race between New England and Nova Scotian schooners. Hearing that this was going on, the Delaware Bay oyster schooners started racing. Originally

The 32ft English Truro River oyster boat *Morning Star*, believed to have been built at Looe in 1812, dredging in the Carrick Roads in 1979. She has a reef down and only a small jib set. *Author*

there was an informal race when 500 schooners went out together at the start of the spring planting season. Later it became more organized with *J & E Riggin* emerging as the local champion. However by the 1930s anything connected with sail was regarded as being antiquated and out of fashion and racing ceased although the 'no power' rule on the Delaware Bay was not lifted until 1945. Because of the stronger tides on the Delaware and difficulties of working up narrow creeks, the oyster schooners were much more seagoing craft. However, like the Chesapeake craft, motor winders were rapidly installed after about 1905.

In Chesapeake Bay racing started with an event held every year on Labor Day at Deal Island from 1924–32. In the inter-war years races for the log canoes at St Michaels were very popular. These one-man single log canoes were used by tonger oystermen until about 1910. When yachtsmen raced them, huge sail areas were set on the tiny canoes. The Deal Island Race was revived in 1960 and was still being held sixteen years later. Another one was started at Sandy Point in 1966 and was also still a popular event ten years later, when the five log brogan *Mustang*, then a yacht, raced in one of the classes. Built at Saxis, Virginia in 1907 her hull was constructed in the true old Chesapeake fashion by fastening five logs together and then hollowing them out. The brogans were actually replaced by bugeyes which in turn were replaced by the skipjacks.

The 1970s races are largely aimed at keeping interest alive in the skipjacks. In spite of considerable efforts to keep them going the numbers of skipjacks have been falling rapidly. In 1974 there were fifty-three skipjacks and one bugeye in the commercial oyster fleet, although not all took out licences that year. Only two years later the numbers had dropped to twenty-seven. Very few have been built since World War II; these are *Helen Virginia* at Crisfield, Maryland 1948, *City of Crisfield*, *Somerset*, and

Mike Parsons on his oyster boat *Leila*, 1969. The mainsheet has the hitch used by the Cornish oystermen for constant adjustment. *Author*

Loraine Rose at Reedville, Virginia 1949, *Caleb W Jones* at Reedville, Virginia 1953, *H M Krentz* at Harryhogan, Virginia 1955, *Rosie Parks* and *Martha Lewis* at Wingate, Maryland 1955 and finally *Lady Katie* at Wingate, Maryland in 1956.

The hulls are mostly getting a bit elderly and many are left in the coves to rot. It is cheaper to build a new tonger than a skipjack. Also the future of oystering is uncertain with pollution in some parts of the Bay and the oyster disease Virus MSX destroying many in the Lower Bay. Even the publicity aimed at helping the working boats has had some side effects which have caused the fleet to thin out faster. The fame of the skipjacks has spread throughout the Eastern United States and many people want to own one. This means that whenever a working oysterman wants to buy a skipjack he is often outbid by yachtsmen and museums. In recent years at least seven skipjacks have been taken out of the working fleet to be on display in museums. The Chesapeake Bay Maritime Museum has a good collection including one of the newer skipjacks, *Rosie Parks*. The carvel planked replica schooner bugeye *J N Carter*, built in 1964 is also kept here. In 1976 the skipjack *Stanley Norman* was having a major refit at the museum ready to go back into dredging but when Captain Roland Pianka of Wenona sold the *Geneva May* that year she went to a museum in Wilmington, North Carolina.

The following skipjacks have all been sold from Deal Island-Wenona area for yachts in the past few years: the *Flora Prince, Maggie Lee, Viola, Mamie Mister, Harry Albough* and then *Annie Lee* although she never reached her owner as she was lost in a storm off the State of Florida. Therefore in the mid-1970s it seemed as if the working skipjacks would be done away with by people wanting to preserve them – in fact killed by kindness.

In the late 1970s however attitudes changed and outside organizations began to contribute to the preservation of these boats. The *Minnie V* was rebuilt at the expense of the City of Baltimore where she spent the summer on display and then in the winter she has been hired out to oystermen for dredging. Melbourne Smith of Annapolis also built a new skipjack, the *Anna McGarvey*. Another new skipjack is the 55ft 25-ton *Dee of St Mary's* built in 1979 over on the west shore of the Chesapeake, at Piney Point; she joined the dredging fleet in 1980.

The individual skipjacks engaged in dredging tend to change over the years but those sold away have almost been replaced by others rejoining the fleet. In 1968 there were thirty-six skipjacks dredging under sail while in 1983 there were twenty-seven. The great threat to skipjacks is not diesel engines, but the oyster disease which in the 1983–84 season was considerably reducing the number of saleable oysters landed.

Three thousand miles away on the other side of the Atlantic there is a similar, although much smaller oyster fishery in Britain. This is in Cornwall, down in the very south-west tip of England where the licences issued by the Truro City Council for oyster dredging in the Fal River and its tributaries forbid the use of power boats. There is also a fairly complex set of regulations by which the dredging can take place, all aimed at striking a balance between earning a living and conserving oyster stocks.

The dredgermen pay to licence each dredge. In the hand-operated 'haul-tow' punts a single man usually uses one dredge, generally in shallow water. The one-man sailboats have two or three dredges while a two-man sailboat has four dredges. In the 1960s one large 30ft Mylor sail boat was working six dredges which seems to be the limit because each dredge has to be hand-hauled and the contents sorted about every five minutes.

Most of the oyster men keep their boats at Flushing, Mylor, Restronguet, Pill and Feock, all on creeks which cut into the hills on the west side of Carrick Roads. From these creeks it is a short sail out to the oyster 'banks' on the edge of the channel which winds some five miles from the Fal River down to the open sea.

The first winter that I went out in a sail boat was in 1969 with Mike Parsons on his 24ft *Leila*. This wooden boat had been built by Mike in 1962 and is a half-decked gaff cutter like all the other work boats. Actually there were a couple of young men trying to dredge with a ketch but they were not being very successful. Nor were a couple from 'up country' (*ie* outside Cornwall) who were dredging with a work boat. The local men made the whole business look much simpler than it really was. To dredge they 'drifted' down wind over the banks by balancing the jib and mainsail. At the end of each drift the boats sailed 'back up' to start again, and they hoped to get about nine drifts in the working time allowed between 9am and 3pm. In order to earn a living the sailboats had to be reasonably fast and very manoeuvrable under sail. On days when it was either a calm or a gale, the boats could not dredge under sail and most of the oyster men turned to normal fishing under power, working a haul-tow punt or some other occupation.

The 31ft *George Glasson* is one of the larger boats and sometimes is worked by three men. She is one of the older boats which was converted from a sea-fishing lugger into an oyster-dredging cutter. The *George Glasson* was bought for £90 paid in gold sovereigns in 1904 and converted from a Mount's Bay half boat by Jim Laity. This boat was passed on to his son and then his grandson, Paul Laity.

Some boats were built specifically for dredging such as the 28ft *Six Brothers* built by William 'Foreman' Ferris beside the creek at Feock in about 1885. Ferris was a very famous Cornish builder, but his only surviving oyster boat seems to be the *Florence*. The 'old' *Six Brothers* was bought by George Vinnicombe in 1953 and he had her rebuilt. In 1968 the *Six Brothers* broke loose from her mooring in a gale and was smashed to pieces at Greatwood Quay, Mylor. The 'new' *Six Brothers* was built as a replacement by Scantlebury at Plymouth in 1969 to a Percy Dalton design.

In the past there does not seem to have been a rigid name for these boats and they were called Restronguet Creek or Truro River oyster boats. In fact these were a shallow draft version of the sailing boats working in East Cornwall. While all the other types have become extinct the Truro River boats have gone on developing. These boats are not part of a preserved tradition, but are totally unique in the western world because they are part of a living tradition.

During the inter-war period a great deal of rebuilding took place to keep boats going, but no new boats were built. However, in 1940 Norman Ferris completed the *Gazelle* at Devoran and then in 1958 he built the *Zephyr* there. At the same time Terry Heard built the 27ft *Result* which was rather narrow because she was built in a garage. Terry Heard soon began operating a boatyard on Mylor Creek and he built the *Crystal Spring*, *Mirre* and *St Meloris* here. These were all wooden-hulled boats which made them rather expensive. To try and make it more feasible for oystermen to buy new boats, Terry Heard switched to using GRP hulls, designed by Percy Dalton. The seven boats built between 1972–78 were all 28ft two-man boats, after which the 23ft

one-man boat hull type was started.

The desire for newer and faster boats has been stimulated by the summer races. There is a long tradition of racing the work boats. In the early years of this century racing was an annual event at Flushing, but now many regattas in the Falmouth area have a class for oyster boats so that they can race nearly every weekend. Since about 1930 the work boats have been going to Fowey Regatta which is about twenty-five miles up the open coast and the furthest the work boats go. They are normally intended for sailing just in sheltered waters.

For racing the boats set topsails and often borrowed light weather sails, off yachts, so that they can round the course under a huge cloud of sail. Since the work boats are

Everard's mulie barge *Britisher* discharging grain at Gleadell's Mills, Morton Corner on the River Trent in 1905. The whole cargo is being unloaded by hand, and a man can be seen carrying a sack ashore.
Gainsborough Library

raced to win, the use of any spinnakers caused a great many rows and in 1974 it was decided to ban them in the Scratch Class and they can now only be used in some Handicap Classes. The final race of the season, started in 1978 as the Silver Oyster Race, is held at Mylor on November 5. This day is an oysterman's holiday to celebrate the winning of a legal battle over their right to use the foreshore free and unrestrained by property owners.

In the races the boats are always called work boats although not every boat is currently owned by a working oysterman. To help control the racing and look after the interests of the oyster dredgers the Falmouth Working Boats Association was formed in the winter of 1978–79.

In October 1979 we counted twenty-one boats dredging in Carrick Roads and were told that one day a record thirty-two boats had all been out. Most of these new boats were worked by young men, although Frank Cock's 32ft *Morning Star*, which according to local legend was built at Looe in 1812, was still dredging.

In 1981 we went out to the fleet with Terry Tuffery in the 24ft *Softwings*, a wooden boat built in 1900 and now maintained by the Cornish Friends of the Maritime Trust. The fleet of twenty-nine was as active as ever and we could pick out the new boats like the 28ft *Agnes*, a ferro-cement hull built in 1979. Other new boats had been built in the 1970s such as the first ferro-cement boat *Blue Circle* in 1975, the wooden *Rhoda Mary* in 1979 and several GRP boats. In fact the fleet was still very active although the recession was biting into incomes and there were fewer plans for new boats than usual. Some building was taking place, notably the *Melita* built in 1832, which was being rebuilt.

The 1982 season started as usual, but before long infected oysters were being

The spritsail barge *Memory* loading grain from a grain machine in the Royal Victoria Dock, London, in 1959. The main trade for the barges was off-loading freights from ships in London and taking them to the small ports. *Patricia O'Driscoll*

Skipper Fred 'Nelson' Wilson and his mate enjoying a joke in the stern cabin of the barge *Centaur* while she was loading bulk sugar at Cliff Quay, Ipswich for London, 1954. The cabin has a table with a horseshoe seat round it and two bunks on either side, behind the panelling. *Nicholas Hardinge*

discovered. Shortly before Christmas it was agreed at a meeting of the oystermen that the fishery should be closed until this disease had worked its way through the stock. In the autumn of 1983 the familiar colourful sight of the working boats was missing from Carrick Roads, although the *Two Sisters*, *Shadow*, *Ada* and *Leila* were being used to work on a private oyster layings.

The Truro River Oyster Fishery of Cornwall and the Maryland Shore of Chesapeake Bay were the only places where fishing remains under sail and only because of artificial situations caused by restrictive regulations. On the east coast of England where the cult around the barges and smacks is so strong, there has been one attempt to revive working sail. This is the wooden 32ft *Ostrea Rose* built in 1980 at Heybridge by Arthur Holt for the Maldon fisherman Michael Emmett. Actually she is worked under power normally and sails are just used in the right conditions.

The last sailing barges trading on the east coast were based in the River Orwell at

The steel mulie (gaff mizzen) barge *Will*, ex-*Will Everard*, could carry up to 280 tons and was one of the largest spritsail barges built. The *Will* was very much a bulk carrier, but barge for barge, the steel hulls are lighter and have less beam than wooden ones and are often faster. *Author*

Ipswich. This busy industrial town seems an unlikely place for the romantic age of sail to end. Actually it was the slowness of the sailing barges which made them useful because grain loaded in the Royal Group of Docks, London, took several days, even weeks, to go 'up and along' the coast to Ipswich. Grain needed at once was sent by motor barge or lorry.

The home of many Ipswich bargemen was Pin Mill, a picturesque little hamlet sheltered by the trees on a bend half way down the River Orwell. Every other cottage in Pin Mill seems to have once been the home of some renowned bargemen. Recently the wheel of the ketch barge *Sussex Belle* was found here which had been bought home by Mo King as a souvenir from the barge when she was wrecked at Great Yarmouth in 1926. Men on the foreshore talk about other barges which have been gone for over a generation, like the ketch barge *Britannia* which is remembered for sailing the 198 miles from Poole to Pin Mill in twenty-two hours at an average of 9 knots.

Sailing coasters only very occasionally made fast passages. Most spent days, even weeks, waiting at anchor for a 'fair wind' to make a passage. A stop at Pin Mill was made all the more welcoming by the presence of the 'Butt & Oyster' on the water's edge at the top of the Hard. The 'Butt' has managed to retain the open tap room and bar of an old country pub and still has genuine ship half models on the walls, a reminder that the coasting trade helped to start many local families in business ventures. The Pin Mill men seem to have avoided working in the big companies but preferred to own their craft. It was the atmosphere of rural simplicity coupled with the fierce seafaring independence that attracted Bob Roberts to come and live here just after World War II.

Bob Roberts was the last man to skipper a sailing barge in the coasting trade. He was a most competent sailor, but his uncompromising attitude often made life ashore very difficult for him. His last barge was the *Cambria* and I remember seeing her in about 1968 coming round Orfordness in fine style into Hollesley Bay with the

The Westcountry sailing barge *Mayblossom* loading road stone at Teluggan Quarry on Lynher River in about 1936. Captain Richard Hosking and his mate are returning aboard. *David Hawker*

The Westcountry sailing barge *Shamrock* restored at Cotehele on the River Tamar in 1979. *Author*

Volendammer Kwakken (large botter) passing through Oranje locks to sell fish at Amsterdam c1900. The botter, with narrow long stern and high bow was the fishing vessel of the Zuiderzee (Ijsselmeer). *Jacob Olie*

bowsprit down and all sails set. No doubt with the fair wind skipper Roberts was hoping to make a fast passage from Yarmouth to London.

The *Cambria* went past the spot in Hollesley Bay where Bob Roberts had, in 1941, abandoned the ketch barge *Martinet* because of a leak started by a bomb in the London docks. Bob Roberts firmly believed that he was rounding off an era. The *Martinet* had been the last ketch barge and then in 1970 his *Cambria* delivered the very last British cargo under sail. But the tradition of sail was too strong to end. There were those who found new ways of keeping barges sailing. Just such a person is Richard Duke who fitted well into Pin Mill's tradition of independent skippers. He had been a master of ocean-going merchantmen before settling at Pin Mill with the sailing barge *Millie*. Richard cannot bear to see old ships (or windmills) rot away. In 1964 he bought the hull of the barge *Centaur* with a partner and rigged her out at Pin Mill so that she could carry passengers. In 1968 he bought the *Convoy*, which had been hit by a ship in Tilbury Dock and was classified as a wreck. Richard took the *Convoy* back to Pin Mill, where a bent steel beam, put in for strength, was removed and the hull sprang back into shape.

The *Convoy*, rigged out as a 'mulie' (gaff mizzen on a spritsail barge) voyaged right round Britain, via the Caledonian Canal. She became one of a new type of sailing vessel which paid her way by making holiday cruises.

Even in the working era some cruise work took place. For instance, on the east coast of England before World War I some barges had their holds swept clean and passengers were taken. The Snape barge *Dawn*, before she was lost off Ramsgate, did this every summer when the grain trade to Snape Maltings fell off. In the 1930s the Maldon barge *Saltcote Belle* took on summer parties which included the writer A P Herbert. At the same time the Finnish shipowner Gustaf Erikson started to carry passengers on his barques on normal commercial voyages. With the steady rise in interest in square riggers, Erikson carried this a step further by sending his four-

In Portugal in 1973 some 200 sailing barges were still active carrying freights from Lisbon inland up the River Tagus. *Author*

Portuguese barges on the River Tagus have no leeboards or centreboards, only the rudder can be lowered by block and tackle to help them sail against the wind. *Author*

masted barque *L'Avenir*, between the annual voyage to Australia, on a summer passenger cruise round the Baltic with his wood-burning tug *Johanna* to tow her into port.

Erikson sold *L'Avenir* so presumably this venture was not a financial success. In the 1930s a few former work boats in the United States and Europe were being used for holiday voyages, but World War II brought an abrupt end to this. In a venture such as Erikson's *L'Avenir* there was a tremendous difference between the skills needed to carry freights and those essential for giving passengers a good holiday.

In the inter-war years Erikson used his hard-headed business sense and the local conditions in the Finnish Åland Islands to run a fleet of large sailing ships as a

The Windjammer
Cruises schooner *Fantome*
off Nevis in the West
Indian Leeward Islands.
Author

commercial venture. Since World War II an American Mike Burke has used a similar approach to operate in the cruise trade the only remaining fleet of privately owned large sailing ships.

In 1947 Captain Mike Burke bought the yacht *Hangover* and began running holiday trips from Miami to the Bahamas. In the daytime Captain Mike and his friends swam and sailed and in the evening they all trailed along to the local bar for a party. This proved popular and Mike Burke, with a great eye for a bargain, realised that large yachts could be bought cheaply and put into the same kind of work. Soon he had the huge 130ft yacht *Polynesia* operating from Miami Beach. When conditions for operating from the United States proved unfavourable, Mike Burke's Windjammer Cruises switched their schooners to St Martin, a West Indies Island in the Leeward Islands and added the 172ft schooner *Yankee Clipper* to the fleet.

Windjammer Cruises remain based at Miami Beach, but their ships operate anywhere people will pay to go, although the West Indies remain the main cruising ground. The schooners are manned on a truly international basis, the masters usually being European because they were less likely to walk out if the going were tough because the air fare home would be more expensive. The deck crews are mostly West Indian, hired and fired as the ships cruise through the islands. The schooners operate from any island which has a good air link with the States. If a local political trouble makes any island too difficult then the schooners simply switch to somewhere else, while back in the States Mike Burke is keeping an eye on the world's largest sailers and buying them up when they come on the market cheaply.

The schooner *John F Leavitt* just before her launching at Thomaston, Maine in 1979. She was the first sailing cargo ship launched in the United States for forty years, but sadly was abandoned in a gale four months later on her maiden voyage when 240 miles off Long Island, and never seen again.
Norman Brouwer

In 1972 when I joined the Windjammer Cruise's four-masted schooner *Fantome* at St Johns, Antigua, for a cruise through the Leeward Islands, their three-masted schooner *Flying Cloud* was operating in the Grenadine Islands, the *Yankee Clipper* was in the Bahamas while the *Polynesia* had been abandoned after a fire the previous year. The total fleet could take over 350 passengers but they were still run on the 'barefoot & casual' basis started by Mike Burke twenty-five years earlier. Anyone could join in with working the *Fantome*, but in practice most of the work was left to the regular crew on such a large ship. It was usual for passengers or 'guests' to take a turn at the wheel, but the whole of the ship's administration was done by Captain Bewley as if it were a yachting trip.

The schooner sailed mostly at night along the chain of the Leeward Islands and anchored each day so that a fresh island could be visited. I thoroughly enjoyed this form of Caribbean Island hopping. In the warm nights one simply lay down and slept on deck which was a tremendous experience to anyone used to the cold grey North Sea. The *Fantome* had been rigged as a staysail schooner, a normal windjammer practice to minimize on sail handling and the engine was kept runing most of the time. However I remember with pleasure being at the wheel one moonlight night in a strong breeze as the huge schooner ploughed through the sea. Most of the guests came because it was an inexpensive cruise, not for the sailing. To them the social activities and shore excursions were the main attraction. It seemed that although the islands were green and beautiful, the meetings between American tourists and the impoverished West Indians sometimes lead to resentment and misunderstandings.

Windjammer Cruises are a unique operation which fit into the holiday market somewhere between the cruise liners and the usual charter boat. The idea of Windjammer Cruises is not to save sailing vessels, but they merely prolong their active life and prove that there is still a place in our technological space age for sail.

In most of the Leeward Island anchorages there were usually a few West Indian trading sloops, but when the *Fantome* anchored in Sandy Bay, Anguilla there were two trading schooners in the Bay and another hauled ashore for a major rebuild. Engines did not appear in the West Indies craft until the 1950s and then in the 1960s there were many United States Navy 6–71 diesel engines auctioned off cheaply and it really looked as if sail was doomed.

Anguilla is a flat dry island which does not favour farming or tourism so the Anguillians, like the men of many other barren lands, have long been forced to go to sea. Anguilla had a large fleet of schooners until the 1950s and they were the last to set down the topmasts and install 'iron topsails' from the US Navy surplus.

Down in the Windward Islands Bridgetown, Barbados used to be a big schooner port. In the 1950s there were usually half a dozen 40–60 ton schooners lying in the careenage at Bridgetown. This dock got its name from 'careening', which is the practice in tideless waters of hauling a vessel down by her mast so that she goes right over, exposing one side below the water line so that it can be worked on. The oldest of the Barbados schooners was the *Warspite*, built in 1918 'inspite of the war', but most were built after World War II. Their main trade was taking goods, imported by steamers into Bridgetown, to the other West Indian Islands. Trade from the Port-of-Spain, Trinidad was much the same and the schooners went right up into Cuba at one time. The inter-island schooners had a strong resemblance to the Grand Bankers which had once come south in the winter to trade in these waters.

In the Windwards Islands the great schooner building centre was the tiny, beautiful island of Bequia in the Grenadines. Although inter-island trade does not seem to support the building of schooners now, 35ft sloops from the Windward Islands still go north with fresh food to St Martins and St Barts or anywhere that tourism has increased the demand. On Bequia, smart open whaling boats are still kept drawn up on the beach. The double-ended, centreboard boats with neatly-stowed lug sails look like museum exhibits, but the meat and cash from ivory sales from the whales are an important local income. In 1982 the Bequian whalers caught four whales.

In the West Indies sail managed to hold its own in the 1970s due to the sudden rise in oil prices. Over on the western side of the Caribbean Sea, Belize also retained many fishing boats and traders who relied only on the Trade Winds for power. Sail power is used commercially in several places in South America and right down south in Chile the island south of Puerto Montt still use gaff sloops. The list of sailing vessels working is still surprisingly long. Many places in the Indian Ocean and throughout Indonesia have men earning their very bare living in wind-powered craft. Working sail in the early 1980s was not dead, but it had certainly been pushed into the background.

CHAPTER 5

New life for old hulls

There is nothing new about people being fascinated by sailing craft. From the earliest times this fascination was revealed by carvings and paintings and the whole history of seafarers has been portrayed in various art forms.

By the nineteenth century most western nations had artists specialising in producing maritime paintings and ship portraits for sailors and an increasingly interested general public. In the Victorian era photographers and writers were starting to record the peak era of sail. This peak was already over by World War I, but this war forced technical and social progress to destroy finally and completely the need for wind-powered ships. In the 1920–30s the fleets of sailing craft became steadily smaller and many creeks and quiet corners of harbours were full of abandoned sailing craft. But there were simply too many craft to preserve every one. Instead, a few interested museums made plans and models of boats from a vanishing age. The actual craft were left to rot away, be cut up for firewood, or continued working under power.

The restoration of actual vessels, when it did start, was usually done for patriotic reasons. In America the wooden sailing frigates *Constellation* and *Constitution* were saved from the scrap yard largely because they were such important reminders of the decades when the United States was still a young country. Periodic bouts of enthusiasm, such as in 1897 when the *Constitution* was 100 years old, led to them being fitted out, but there was no long term plan for preservation.

In the early 1920s, in Britain, there was a great outcry when the Royal Navy thought of breaking up HMS *Victory*, a ship which had become a national legend because she was Nelson's flagship at the decisive Battle of Trafalgar in 1805. The *Victory* was a largely rotting hulk laying off Portsmouth Naval Dockyard, but the Society for Nautical Research became responsible for steering her course back to a fully-rigged ship, open to the public.

The idea of saving famous ships had taken root and this led to the American whaling ship *Charles W Morgan*, a bluff bowed old-timer dating from 1841, being preserved in Mystic, Connecticut. From this project grew an entire collection of American craft and these are now kept near a whole neighbourhood of historic houses which make up Mystic Seaport Museum.

All forms of preservation came to an abrupt halt with World War II and the post-war material shortage which followed it. However, preservation got going again when the clipper *Cutty Sark* was towed to a dry dock at Greenwich, London in 1954, Since then most major seaports have been acquiring and preserving a square rigger, while New York has a couple in the four-masted barque *Peking* and the full rigged ship *Wavertree*.

These museum ships are a result of civic pride and tremendous effort by individual sailing ship enthusiasts. Some projects collapse, but others achieve the near impossible. Such a project involved the British barque *Elissa*, built in 1877 and only 400 tons – minute by modern merchant ship standards, but a huge vessel to restore. Nevertheless at Galveston, Texas she was totally rebuilt and actually sailed again in 1982.

To survive, sailing ships have to have a purpose. Nearly all large museum ships give service to the community by providing an informative tourist attraction. With smaller craft, they can be rebuilt and go on sailing. This of course is a more worthwhile exercise and nearer to their original purpose. There are far too many old ships tied up to quays.

When sailing working craft first came on the market cheaply in the 1920–30s many were bought for conversion to yachts. They were always altered from their original appearance. Certain types were so close to yachts that they were eagerly sought after. In the United States the Friendship sloops – the gaff sloops used for lobstering from Friendship, Maine – were great favourites, while in Britain, the Bristol Channel pilot cutters were much admired. The pilot cutters were popular because of their good sea-keeping qualities, and were not too expensive to maintain. The Colin Archer-designed sailing rescue ship from Norway was another popular type, although they were slow sailers and their heavy rolling action sometimes drove their crews to despair.

The first rescue ship built in Norway to go out with the fishing fleet was the ketch *Colin Archer* in 1893. She is now preserved and fulfils a useful role by being sailed by club members. Probably the first club to be formed to offer its members a chance to sail on a traditional craft was the Thames Barge Sailing Club in 1948. Since then the Club has sailed on the 'sprittie' barges *Spurgeon*, *Arrow*, *Asphodel*, *Westmoreland*, and now *Pudge* and *Centaur*.

The Norfolk Wherry Trust was formed in 1949 to restore the wherry *Albion* back to cargo-carrying under sail on the East Anglian Broads. These wherries have a single gaff sail, rather like the American Cat Boats, so that they could sail up the narrow rivers which link the Broads (shallow lakes) that form the Broadland. The *Albion* managed a few freights but in the end had to revert to summer holiday charter to help to pay for the cost of maintenance.

The Norfolk Wherry Trust managed to keep their wherry sailing over a long period of time which is a considerable achievement because many such schemes quietly died once the initial enthusiasm was over. The Trust have stuck rigidly to the claim that *Albion* was the 'last wherry', when in fact there were several still working as power craft and about forty lying around derelict. It was not until 1981 that Vincent and Linda Pargeter raised the 60ft *Maud* from Ranworth Broad with the aim of restoring her.

Vincent Pargeter had originally been sailing on the barge *Convoy* with Richard Duke, but Vincent, who restores windmills for a living, was well aware that an eighty-year-old barge hull was likely to need a major rebuild. Given the amount of work needed to rebuild an 80ft barge, he turned instead to a wherry, finally picking on the *Maud* which had been sunk in 1976 to reduce erosion on a bird reserve.

The *Maud* is a typical double-ended clinker trading wherry, unlike the *Albion* which is unusual in being the only carvel-built wherry. The *Maud* was built in 1899 by Hall at Reedham and the pleasure wherry *Hathor* and wherry yacht *Lady Edith* built by him are still afloat. The pleasure wherries were built for summer holiday cruises. They had the same hulls as the trading wherries while the wherry yachts had the same rig but carvel hulls and counter sterns. The wherry yacht *Olive* is back carrying holiday charters.

As the years roll by we all realise that it is not just the craft that we are having to preserve, but the skills in maintaining them. The Thames spritty barges have survived in enough numbers for the whole tradition around them to survive and it is worth a brief survey to see how prevailing attitudes have effected this preservation.

The barges were at their peak around 1900 when around 2000 where trading. They were built to earn their owners and crews a living by providing cheap transport and competed mainly against the railways. The barges have flat bottoms but the larger ones could still make long coastal passages. The average barge could load around 120–150 tons, but thanks to the ingenious use of winches, only needed a crew of two to handle the sails.

Barges were built in sufficient numbers for a great deal of experimentation in hull shape to take place. These barges were in an extremely competitive world and the bargemen were notorious in their enthusiasm to 'race' to be first in port to get the

The Norfolk Broads trading wherry *Cornucopia* was built in 1893 at Stalham. The single gaff sail was ideal for these inland waterways.

The Norfolk wherry had a double-ended clinker hull. The pleasure wherry was the same although they were built to carry summer passengers, while the wherry yachts, like the *Olive*, here on the River Ant, were carvel hull and counter stern. *Author*

Renewing planks on the trading ketch *Emily Barratt* at Cook's, Maldon, 1983. Between the frames the 'salt trays' can still be seen which were packed with rock salt as a wood preservative when she was built in 1913. *Author*

next 'turn' for a freight.

When the engines first came in the bargemen were not very keen on them because a sprittie properly handled could sail up narrow creeks or across the North Sea and the early engines – which were low powered and unreliable – were not much help. After World War II this attitude changed as the skipper and mate worked to share the freight money with the owners and they wanted engines so that they could share the post-war freight boom. By the 1950s it was obvious that barges working under sail only could only last a few more years. Apart from the Ipswich grain barges, little money was spent for long-term maintenance on barge hulls and if they failed the load line survey then owners sold them off for yachts or houseboats.

In the 1950s a group of young men came into barging with a burning ambition to keep dozens of barges working under sail as long as possible. Everyone knew this was the bitter end of cargo-carrying under sail and they delighted in reviving old ways and doing everything under sail.

In the mid-1950s I briefly experienced this nostalgic period as third hand on the *Will Everard* trading to Hull and then in 1956 as mate with Peter Light on *Xylonite* in trade between London and Mistley. Barging, especially in the winter, was a very hard life and when under way we were often sailing for long periods which could be exhausting. These were followed by long and frustrating delays waiting to load in the docks or at anchor 'windbound' waiting for a fair wind to make a passage. Barges rarely sailed against the tide in the Thames Estuary so that the tide and wind completely ruled your life.

We seemed to have little in common with even the motor barge crews and very little with the people ashore, but there was a wonderful sense of comradeship between the remaining sailormen. The young skippers keeping the barges going were Jim Lawrence on *Memory*, Mick Lungley on *Marjorie*, Pat Fisher on *May* and John Fairbrother on *Spinaway C*. These were all in the London-Ipswich grain trade while

At Maldon is the partly-restored Gravesend bawley *Lilian* built in 1869 and the rigged *Marigold*, a replica of the *Lilian*. Note the sweeps (oars) carried in the lumber irons. *Author*

Xylonite was owned by Horlocks of Mistley who still had another sailing barge, the *Portlight*. We saw a lot of *Portlight*'s skipper, Gordon Hardy, and hours were spent in her panelled cabin talking about such matters as whether barges would last after trading finally ended.

No one wanted to see the brown-sailed barges vanish, but as yachts they only had a limited future. This problem had, in 1956, prompted the formation of the Sailing Barge Trust, closely modelled on the Norfolk Wherry Trust, which bought the *Memory* and kept her in trade until 1960 when she was laid up. A year later she was sold to private owners and started taking trips from Mill Beach, Heybridge, in Essex. Because the barge did not have an engine she was replaced with *Thalatta* and this project grew into the East Coast Sail Trust, a youth training scheme, which now also operates the barge *Sir Alan Herbert*, ex-*Lady Jean*.

Back in the 1960s when *Memory* was laid up at Lower Halstow the first attempt at running a barge for holiday cruises was tried out at Maldon, Essex. This was on *Marjorie* after she was bought out of trade and converted for luxury cruising. This venture was a non-starter, but gradually it was discovered the type of holiday best suited to barges. It had to be on an informal basis, particularly for young people who liked to be in groups, and had little cash to spend. However every skipper-owner has had to develop their own particular form of charter work.

It took some of the skippers who had been used to freights of timber, wheat and sunflower seed, several years to adjust to the needs of people on holiday charters. Sailing barges are remarkably versatile and were soon adapted to this new form of charter. Maldon, an old estuary port with an attractive waterfront and even more attractive as a quay where barges could berth for a modest fee, became the centre of this new charter work. By the mid-1960s the *Marjorie* was making frequent holiday voyages, while *Kitty*, *Lord Roberts* and *Dawn* were all rigged out and were put into the charter trade to meet expenses. In order to keep up with their schedules and get the

The elm deck pump, a 10ft long hollow tube to the bilge, being fitted to the replica ketch *Nonsuch*, at Appledore, Devon. 1968. *William Mallinson & Sons*

Fred Schofield on the Humber Keel *Annie Maud* at York, 1976. Fred Schofield was responsible for much of the knowledge given for re-rigging the keel *Comrade* and the sloop *Amy Howson*, but sadly the *Annie Maud* restoration failed and she was broken up. *Author*

charterers back on time, most barges were fitted with engines, but John Fairbrother insisted on doing the whole trip under sail. He had been a skipper of the *Spinaway C* trading to Ipswich with grain before he rigged out the *Kitty*. Most barges either used an engine or a small tug to get up the narrow channel to Maldon's Hythe Quay, but John Fairbrother would bring the *Kitty* in under sail, just as the barges had done in the old days.

For individual owners, even with the help of charter work, it is a struggle to find the finance to keep a barge sailing. Increasingly it has become the company-owned barges, which have had more money spent on them, that have a better chance of survival under sail for future generations to see. Of the companies which had sailing barges in trade, only Crescent Shipping with *Sirdar* and then *Cabby* and Pauls with *Ena* have kept a barge sailing. The first barge bought by a company in the revival era was the *May* which was bought by a subsidiary of the sugar giants, Tate & Lyle. She carried some cargoes under sail and although fitted with an engine she might lay claim to being the last trading barge with sails. However, most companies that buy barges have been using them for promoting good staff and customer relations.

The international container company OCL bought the steel barge *Will* and they send her all over north-west Europe promoting their operations, while Bell's Whisky used to charter different barges to go round the coast of Britain visiting ports and sometimes piers such as Brighton. At each destination they hold parties for their customers. Bell's eventually bought the barge *Hydrogen*, built at Rochester in 1906 as a spritsail barge, but was the last former sailing barge trading as a motor barge. In 1981 she made her first promotion voyage after being re-rigged.

While most charter barges keep in the Thames Estuary, the company promotion

barges often visit ports all over north west Europe. The *Redoubtable*, under the name *David Gestetner*, actually ended up abandoned in 1982 in Norway after getting into difficulties on a promotion voyage to the Shetland Isles. Considering this wooden barge was sixty-seven years old and had only been intended to trade between London and Great Yarmouth, this was a fairly ambitious voyage to send her on. However, fitted with engines, company barges are fairly common visitors to continental ports such as Amsterdam which of course regularly saw sailing barges before World War II.

While about sixty barges have found a new lease of life, the Essex and Whitstable smacks which hail from the same coast around the Thames have also managed to survive. These smacks were either trawling or stowboating between the Thames Estuary sandbanks or dredging oysters in the rivers. They are fast and handy and with their gaff cutter rig make excellent yachts. However in the 1930s Hervey Benham and Michael Frost thought it was a pity to see the West Mersea oyster smacks converted to yachts and thought they should instead be left unaltered and taken out fishing, even if it was only on an amateur 'free food' basis.

Hervey Benham sailed the 11-ton *Charlotte*, built by the well-known smack builder Aldous at Brightlingsea, for several years, while Michael Frost was very taken with the *Boadicea*. He found her while rowing through the smacks one day in the rain, and this lead to him eventually buying her in 1938 and having a lifetime's love affair with this little smack which has now been going on for almost fifty years.

While most of the Essex smacks have counter sterns, so typical of the vessels of Victorian Britain, the *Boadicea* had a transom of an earlier era. No one knew the origin of *Boadicea* until Hervey Benham discovered, while searching through customs records of Maldon, that she had been built in that estuary port in 1808.

In the summer the smacks sailed for pleasure made enough entries to keep the annual West Mersea Smack Race going. This event became so popular that other fishing villages revived their smack races and this gave a new reason for keeping the smacks going. But the problem was that most of the smacks had been around for about seventy years and their hulls were distinctly tired. Many years of towing fishing gear usually resulted in the counter sterns sagging down (in the case of the *Quiz* it had almost sagged to water level!), while wear and decay had destroyed many of the covering boards, where the sides met the decks. The list of defects in hulls was usually a long one. Indeed, if it had not been for the plentiful supply of good quality timber in the late Victorian and Edwardian era, these vessels would not have lasted that long.

One of the first smacks to come ashore for a total rebuild was the *Boadicea*. By 1970 the new hull was almost complete and not a single piece of wood remained from the original hull, but the hull shape remained exactly the same. Since then most smacks have had a 'rebirth'. The 42ft *Charlotte Ellen* has been rebuilt twice for John Rigby, once when she was converted back to sail from a motor fishing vessel, and again after she was wrecked on a Thames Estuary sandbank.

Racing has become one of the main functions for these restored smacks with Dick Harman's Brightlingsea based *ADC* and the West Mersea *Hyacinth* emerging as the new champions. The *Charlotte Ellen* was re-rigged with the same sized sail area as the *ADC*, although her hull is a little smaller, with the intention of beating the *ADC*. This did not quite work out so John Rigby bought the 49ft *Sunbeam* and had her rebuilt by Johnnie Milgate at Peldon Creek, Essex. The *Sunbeam* appears to have been built back in the 1870s and is remembered working under sail in the 'stowboat' (sprat) fleet from Brightlingsea in the 1920s, but legend has it that she had been a crack racer in the Victorian smack races.

Regrettably, although there are about forty smacks, many of them like the West Mersea *Peace* and *Gracie* sticking rigidly to the traditional deck layout and sail plan, the fishing side of the revival has almost died out. However during the early 1980s Donald Rainbird's *Mayflower* was still carrying and using nets, while Dick Norris' Whitstable smack *Stormy Petrel* had a trawl and used her for dredging sometimes on free oyster grounds.

One of the fascinations of restoring a traditional working boat is discovering how they handle under sail. When my son wanted a boat we had the 15ft Suffolk beach boat *Pet* restored which had been lying derelict on a beach at Thorpeness from where she had been fished. Although we did not understand many of the features in the hull she was rebuilt as near as possible to the way she had been when ex-ship's carpenter Bill Bugg originally built her in 1902.

The *Pet* had the two-masted lug rig used by thousands of British inshore fishing boats before the introduction of petrol engines, yet the first time we tried to sail her she proved to be an unmanageable brute. Obviously we had a lot to learn so we talked to retired Southwold fishermen who had begun in this type of clinker-built transom sterned boat and all the little knacks of how to handle a lugger began to dawn on us.

Tryggen Larsen on the Norwegian jakt *Brodrene*, built about 1840 and rebuilt in 1906. The rail is being replaced in further rebuilding in 1979. The windlass is turned by hand with spikes placed in square holes in the barrel end. *Author*

After the mast, stays and sails, the most important gear of a sailing vessel was the windlass because they often had to anchor 'windbound' in bad weather. This well-cared-for hand windlass is on the Danish custom cutter *Viking. Author.*

The final mastery came when we left the outboard at home and went out fishing under sail and oar. When we used her as a work boat the *Pet* came alive and every detail in the simple hull and rigging showed a clear practical purpose.

In sailing *Pet*, even for just a little part time fishing, we derived tremendous personal satisfaction, as well as a lot of herring. I thought back to Gordon Hardy who was skipper of the sailing barges *George Smeed* and *Portlight* in their final years of trading and how he used to say he could never sail for pleasure, that there had to be a practical reason for making so much effort to arrive at your destination. Graham Hussey, who sailed with Gordon, also seems to have become immersed in the mid-1950s dream of continuing to work under sail and is restoring the 19ft Yarmouth shrimper *Horace & Hannah* for day fishing under sail, the purpose she was built for in 1908.

To continue sailing any form of traditional craft a useful role must be found. The number of people aft, and the extra chimney in the deck, tells that the sailing barge *Marjorie* is on charter, 1973. *Author*

Bill Coke mending a sail on the Swedish customs cutter *L'Atalanta*, built as the *Ran* in 1904 by Gustaffsson at Landskrona. *Author*

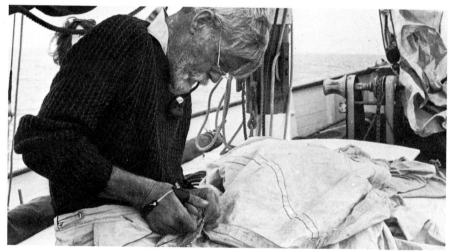

Fishermen are usually extremely surprised when someone comes along and restores one of their worn-out and obsolete craft. In purely practical terms it is easier to build new boats, but replicas lack the authenticity of the real article and are frequently inaccurate. Although owning a traditional boat is a ,fulfilment of a personal dream, anyone taking a romantic view of this type of craft is heading for a disappointment. There is an enormous amount of hard work in maintaining and sailing a traditional vessel. There are simply no short cuts: a Viking longship replica or restored nineteenth century fishing smack have their limitations, and one either accepts this or moves on to some other phase of life.

It is impossible to make the clock stand still and technical progress, for better or worse, marches relentlessly on. In a way this makes it more important to maintain traditional craft because they are such a strong link with the basic realities of life.

Traditional boats were built by men with their hands to be powered by the elements.

It would be a mistake to allow the remaining traditional boats to become museum exhibits or very pretty yachts, but as we grow further from the age of working sail how is an understanding of their real purpose to be retained? In the 1970s in the Netherlands this question was tackled very seriously and competitions started in which one day a year the botters and other fishing boats go out fishing, while the sailing cargo-carrying barges raced with 'stront' (farmyard manure) from Friesland across the Ijsselmeer to Noord Holland province. This theme was taken a step further when non-profit making societies re-opened the Kromhout Ship Yard, Amsterdam and the Zwolsman Werf (yard) at Workum in Friesland solely for traditional craft. The effect of the world recession on the Netherlands' economy has meant that both yards have had to abandon their purely traditional approach and become ordinary commercial yards in order to survive. At least a worthwhile attempt has been made to continue repairing and running craft in the traditional manner. In 1983 there were no less than 206 craft, mostly traditional sailing craft, operating holiday charters in the Netherlands. The largest of these was Harry 'The botter king' Smit's barquentine *Elizabeth Smit* which was running trips on the Ijsselmeer from near the Central Station, Amsterdam. Most of the Dutch craft are based at Hoorn and Enkhuizen, lovely old red brick towns which were merchant centres long before Amsterdam and Rotterdam grew to be great commercial centres. In the winter when all the craft have returned from voyages on the Ijsselmeer and the Baltic, the quays at Enkhuizen are lined with fishing botters, schooners and every type of fore-and-aft craft.

Many of the traditional craft in the Netherlands are small enough to be privately-owned such as the steel tjalk *Roelofje* at Durgerdam, an attractive dyke village perched on the seawall near Amsterdam. The *Roelofje* was built in 1902 to trade in peat from Friesland across to the towns in the Sea Provinces. She was crewed by the family owning her, father, mother and girls sleeping in the aft cabin while the boys slept in

One way to use a restored craft is to continue its original function. The Suffolk beach boat *Pet* does some fishing under sail and here in 1983 the beam trawl is being hauled. *Pearl Simper*

Sailing craft can usually be relied on to attract publicity. Here the ancient custom of the Mayor of Colchester hauling the first of the season's oysters takes place aboard an Essex smack in 1973.

A pleasure boat loaded with trippers returning to Brighton beach in about 1905. Boats worked off open beaches at hundreds of places round the coast of Britain.

the tiny forepeak. One of these boys later took over as skipper and during World War II took an entire freight of silver from the Amsterdam banks to a hiding place in Friesland to prevent them being seized by the Nazis. The skipper was a notoriously silent man, but as the tjalk could load just over 100 tons it must have been a memorable freight. The *Roelofje*'s other modest claim to fame is that she was one of the last trading under sail, until 1965 when Gijs van Gortel bought her for a yacht.

One of the strange facts is that all these revival movements in Britain and the Netherlands grew up quite independently, largely unaware that anyone was doing the same thing in other countries, at least until the mid-1970s when publicity in magazines on boat restoration made everyone aware of what was happening in all western maritime countries.

In Denmark the age of wooden cargo vessels and the era of restoring traditional craft overlapped. In the 1930s motor galease (ketches) were still being built in Denmark for Greenland and trade in the Baltic islands, but at the same time a programme of building road bridges was introduced. This programme was delayed by World War II so that wooden motor sailers went on being built into the 1940s. The Danish inter-island trade finally declined in the late 1960s and dozens of wooden 'Baltic traders' came on to the market relatively cheaply. For about a decade there was a steady stream of wooden motor schooners and galease going through the North Sea bound on adventure voyages and charter operations, mostly under new British, American, Canadian, Dutch, German and French owners.

The best-known yard for restoring wooden traders is J Ring Andersen's at Svendborg on the Baltic island of Fyn in southern Denmark. The walls of Ring Andersen's offices are lined with the half models of numerous ships built here. Many of these traders had jagt-built hulls with round bows and sloping transoms. In 1938 Ring Andersen launched a totally different type, the 98ft galease *Havet* with a 'helpmotor'. She was built for Karl Lorentzen, who as a boy had run away to sea in a German full rigged ship, and then spent some time in the Gloucester Grand Bankers. These schooners were the inspiration behind *Havet* (Ocean) which has a counter stern

and curved bows, but a shoal draft for the Baltic. Ring Andersen built a series of *Havet* hulls finishing with the *Mona* in 1951. They also converted many schooners to motor vessels and then, when the era finished, converted them back to sail for adventure voyages.

On the south shore of Svendborg Sound is the island of Taasing and here, at Troense, Michael Kiersgaard revived the Jacobsens Plads as a wooden ship repair yard. Kiersgaard had begun by restoring the 18ft smakkejolle *Charles*, an open fishing boat built in about 1880 at Elsinore, but his restless nature caused him to move on to larger craft and then into charter work in the former fish carrier *Otto Mathiassen* and then the steel schooner *Midsommer*. At Jacobsens Plads several schooners, which other Danish yards had said were impractical to restore, have been totally rebuilt. In the winter of 1983–84 the yard was rigging the *Kaskelot* as a barque. While trees grown on the island of Fyn were shaped into masts and spars for the *Kaskelot*, they gave off the wonderful sweet timber smell which is so much a part of a traditional shipyard.

Another centre of schooner-owning in southern Denmark was Marstal, but since it is on the isolated island of Aerö it has no schooners now. However the island of Langeland is now linked to the rest of Denmark by a bridge and the main port, Rudkøbing has attracted restored craft. In about 1982 owners with boats at Rudkøbing decided to form an association to make it easier for those who could not afford the shipyard costs of restoring a wooden vessel. The association was the result of two ideas coming together – one to restore wooden craft and the other to preserve the town's ornate warehouse on the harbour.

Each member has a space in the packing warehouse to store gear and there is a bandsaw, joiner and planer which members can make use of as well as the slipway on the harbour. A ship's carpenter and iron worker help with the more complicated jobs, but the general idea is for members to do their own shipwrighting and also help each other.

The Rudkøbing association is one of the occasional incidents of local government authorities helping with cash and support for traditional ship restoration. Another

The 28ft Hastings beach boat *Edward & Mary* hauled ashore ready for restoration by Steve Peak at Hastings near the place where she was built as an auxiliary two-masted lugger in 1919. The beamy clinker hull was developed for bringing heavy catches through the breaking waves. *Author*

A rare surviving bar capstan on the beach at Worthing, 1984. Capstans were used to haul decked luggers ashore at Worthing, Brighton, Eastbourne, and Hastings during the nineteenth century. *Author*

instance of local government promoting ship restoration is at the German North Sea port of Bremerhaven. The city of Bremen at the head of the River Weser used to be the major port for north-west Germany, but as ships grew larger the modern port of Bremerhaven grew up near the mouth of the Weser. Bremerhaven is a great commercial success, but like many modern towns it is a little sensitive about its lack of 'heritage'.

In 1977 the enterprising authorities of Bremerhaven held a 'Windjammer-treffen' (rally) there and saw that traditional ships attracted public attention. To keep this interest going the Schiffergilde (skipper's guild) was formed the following year and the Finkenwerder fishing kutter *Astarte* was restored. Also the National Maritime Museum (Deutsches Schiffahrtsmuseum) was opened and they restored the square topsail cutter *Grönland* (Greenland). The Schiffergilde went on to encourage other owners to bring their craft to Bremerhaven for restoration. A quay and adjoining workshop was made available to members of the guild and equally important, cash grants were made to genuine restoration projects. Craft being restored at Bremerhaven by guild members include the Portuguese salt schooner *Vale de Moura* of Setubal, the Norwegian Colin Archer cargo ketch *Rakel* and the English smack *Nellie & Leslie* of Boston.

It seems very creditable that these generous restoration projects should have received grants of public money. After all in western Europe most governments help to support sport and the arts, so why not traditional craft restoration?

While Bremerhaven has helped in the restoration of craft from all over Europe, the Museumshafen Oevelgoenne at Hamburg was opened in 1977 largely with the aim of encouraging the restoration of the ewer, a barge used for fishing and cargoes on the River Elbe. This novel idea of using the small harbour at Oevelgoenne as a place where only well-restored craft could be kept was championed by Egon Heinemann (1933–83) who owned a printing works and as a side line started a publishing house dealing specially in German nautical subjects. Heinemann's enthusiasm helped to fan on the great upsurge of interest in traditional craft in Germany during the late 1970s.

The traditional windlass for hauling boats up a slipway is still used in Zwolsman Werf, Workum in Friesland, North Netherlands, 1978. *Author*

The Zwolsman Werf was reopened by a society for rebuilding Dutch craft in 1977. Here the botter *BU61* and wieringeraak *WK44* are seen hauled out in 1978. *Author*

Heinemann published a book on ewers by Joachim Kaiser whose unlimited enthusiasm for these barges lead him to be called the 'Ewer Pope'. Joachim moved on to being fascinated by steel schooners which were built in large numbers in the northern province of the Netherlands. In Germany, as in Denmark, the state will pay boat owners to take 'young people with social problems' on voyages. However young people sometimes find just sailing from A to B rather pointless and to give some purpose to his voyages Joachim Kaiser bought a steel Dutch motor coaster to carry cargoes under sail. He fitted this vessel out at Gluckstadt, a little port on the Elbe, as the schooner *Undine*.

The shortage of timber in the Netherlands saw steel craft being built before World War I but the Groningen *Zeehond* is the only surviving wooden tjalk. She was wrecked here crossing the Zuiderzee in 1888 and now, due to polder building, is sitting miles inland in a field. *Author*

The panelled cabin of the steel tjalk *Roelofje* just as the barge family left her, complete with 'tafflkleed' (table carpet). *Author*

The number of ways and schemes in western Europe to keep traditional ships sailing seem to be endless, but there is little doubt that the United States now has more traditional craft than any other country. This started in the inter-war year period when small fishing and trading schooners could be bought cheaply and used for passenger cruises on sheltered waters of the eastern seaboard.

The older sail-trained sailors who had been brought up to fight the North Atlantic in all weathers, were greatly amused by these 'cattle boats' or 'dude' schooners, as they called them. The word 'dude' came from the American West where it was an uncomplimentary term for a tourist. However, the 'dude' cruise trade has given a handful of smaller schooners a way of surviving and this has given many people an enjoyable taste of life under sail.

The cruise trades relationship with officialdom has gone through some bad patches. For a long time the US Coast Guard assumed that the cruise schooners were a passing phase and as the ships rapidly grew older the whole business would quietly fade away. The regulations were simply left so that any American ship under 100 tons could carry passengers providing they were not fitted with an engine. Once an engine was fitted then the safety regulations were so severe that it was virtually impossible for them to operate under the American flag. This suited everyone and the schooners all carried a power yawl slung, in true Yankee fashion, in the stern davits. These were lowered and used to push under the counter sterns or tow from ahead.

Almost all the cruise schooners are still pure sailers aided by yawls, but the Coast Guard were forced to turn their attention to the cruise trade after the loss of the Chesapeake Ram schooner *Levin J Marvel* in 1954. Between 1889–1911 numerous flat-bottomed, centreboard three-masted schooners known as 'rams' were built to trade through the canal linking the Chesapeake and Delaware. Several of these were used in the Chesapeake Bay for cruising from the 1930s until the *Levin J Marvel* was lost. The Coast Guard now came under pressure to produce regulations to involve themselves in the passenger windjammer fleet.

This started in 1958; only a year later there was a fresh outcry when the passenger-carrying *Albatross* went down with loss of life in the Gulf of Mexico. To remain on station in the temperamental North Sea craft had to be able to stand up to some very rugged conditions; this steel vessel had been built as a German pilot schooner, but at the time of her loss she had been converted to a brigantine which meant more spars and weight aloft.

Briefly in 1964 there was a period when the Coast Guard said that all passenger-licenced sailers must be able to take a knock-down blow so that if the masts went right over into the water, the vessel would still right herself. To expect 90 degrees of positive stability is quite a lot to ask from any ship, but it was revealed later that the Coast Guard's own New London based training barque the *Eagle* only possessed a mere 82 degrees stability. Officialdom had now to come to terms with the realisation that commercial sailing vessels actually existed in the space age. Now every cruise schooner has to pass a Coast Guard inspection every year.

Maine has become an important centre for the cruise trade because its coast has enough sheltered water and unspoilt towns and islands to sail in picturesque scenery to a different anchorage most days. In 1966 there seem to have been nine schooners carrying passengers and a decade later the number of cruise ships on the north eastern seaboard had increased to twenty although two of these, the 58ft *Richard Robbin Jr* and the 76ft *J & E Riggin* were hauled out at Rockland, Maine and were being rebuilt. These were once part of a huge fleet of schooners which had dredged oysters in Delaware Bay. Actually the oldest craft on the American register, the Delaware clam boat *Cashier* built in 1841 also started out as an oyster schooner. Another old timer which has not been so lucky is the 67ft centreboard schooner *Australia*. She was built in 1862 and finally ended up at Mystic Seaport Museum, but her hull seems to have reached the point of no return and they simply have a decaying shell on display.

Actually the original building date and hull shape are about the only features which stay with the craft throughout her life, other features such as name, trade and actual timbers changing as the years roll by. In fact many former working craft hulls are actually growing younger as more new wood is put into them. With the cruise trade expanding there were not enough reasonably sound large schooners left to convert,

The handspike windlass and grapple anchor on the Dutch fishing blazer *TX 33* before she was badly damaged by fire in 1979. The blazer was built for fishing off the coast and had higher sides than the botter. *Author*

so several new craft have been built on traditional lines, starting with the 88ft centreboard schooner *Mary Day* in 1962. She is one of four superb wooden ships built by Harvey F Gamage at South Bristol, Maine. Next, in 1964, came the 114ft *Shenandoah*, a topsail schooner built on the lines of the revenue cutter *Joe Lane* of 1849. In fact *Shenandoah* is a full scale replica of a Baltimore clipper, a type which greatly influenced western sailing ship design. The other two, *Bill of Rights* and the *Harvey Gamage*, were built on the same lines, but without square topsails on the foremast and instead had gaff topsails on both masts. Like Baltimore clippers, however, the masts are raked aft which, it was then believed, but now much debated, produced more speed.

The *Shenandoah* was intended to take twenty-nine passengers with a crew of six. In 1967 the 100ft steel auxiliary schooner *Mystic Whaler* was built at Tarpon Springs, Florida to take forty-four passengers and a permanent crew of four. Another new schooner is the ferro-cement 'sailing sidewalk' *Rachael & Ebenezer*, built on the site of Percy & Small Yard, Bath in 1972. She got her name through someone looking through an old British newspaper of the sailing ship era and coming on an article where a writer said that all American ships had names like *Rachael & Ebenezer*.

The main centre for the cruise schooners is Camden, Maine. Here in the fall of 1976 and in other ports around Penobscot Bay the schooners were cocooned in plastic 'houses' for the winter. All were built for very different work. At Camden were the cargo schooners 72ft *Mattie* and 71ft *Mercantile*, the 88ft Boston pilot schooner *Roseway*, the exploration schooner *Bowdoin*, the *Mary Day* and the 118ft Gloucester fisherman *Adventure*. Built in 1926 she was the last of the schooners built at James Yard, Essex and represents the final stage of development in that she is a 'knockabout' schooner. These didn't have the dangerous 'widow-making' bowsprits. The fleet had increased so that the Portland, Maine pilot schooner *Timberwind* and the oldest schooner, the 63ft *Stephen Taber* built in 1871, were spending the winter just along the coast at the jetty at Rockport.

After Camden, Rockland had the largest fleet with the *Isaac Evans*, *Lewis R French*, *Rachael & Ebenezer* and the only three-masted American trading schooner left sailing, the 132ft *Victory Chimes*. She took this name from a Nova Scotian schooner which was built at the time the Victory Chimes of World War I rang out. The present *Victory Chimes* joined the Maine cruise fleet in 1954; she is actually the only surviving Chesapeake Ram and was built as the *Edwin & Maud* in 1900. The *Victory Chimes* is owned by Captain Fred Guild (rhymes with wild). He has actually been in the cruise work since 1932. During World War II he was doing anti-submarine patrol work under sail, which included commanding the former Grenfell Mission schooner *Jessie Goldthwait*. On returning home he went back into the leisure cruise work, bought the *Stephen Taber* in 1945, but found she was not really big enough to support a wife and four children so two years later he purchased the fishing schooner 72ft *Alice S Wentworth*, built in 1863. The following year the schooner *Grace & Alice* was acquired making three schooners sailing under the Guild houseflag. At the end of the 1950 season the *Stephen Taber* was sold and the following winter vandals stripped the laid-up *Grace & Alice* of fittings so that it was impossible to send her back to work again.

The *Alice S Wentworth* left the Maine cruise trade in 1961 and eventually became part of a Boston restaurant. There is no surer way of making certain that an old ship finally dies than by turning her into a restaurant. The *Alice S Wentworth* was no exception to this rule, but long before this, Captain Guild had gone as Master of *Victory Chimes* and finally bought her in 1959. As befitted the largest commercial sailing ship under the American flag the schooner glistened with new paint, bright clear varnish and gold leaf. This spotless appearance is appreciated by the passengers although they take little part in the sailing of the ship. The crew of six are ruled by Captain Guild who expects every detail to be done properly. Other traditions of sail are also observed like the mate being addressed as Mr Mate, however youthful he may be. Another member of the crew is the donkey-man who lives forward next to the auxiliary 'donkey engine'. The engine is used for hauling the anchor, an important

The Dutch steel klipper *Avontuur* built in 1909, first engined in 1925 and sails removed in 1952 before being rigged out again in 1980, a familiar pattern of events for both Dutch and English barges. She has kept the original single-masted rig but whether the gaff is curved or straight seems to be owner's preference. *Author*

feature on a vessel which anchors every night. Also there is a yawl boat to push the engineless *Victory Chimes* into port. The *Victory Chimes* has accommodation for forty-three passengers and like the other Maine schooners sails on a weekly basis and returns to port every weekend for new guests.

The rest of the cruise schooners are spread out in the New England ports to the south. The *Shenandoah* sails out of Martha's Vineyard, *Bill of Rights* from Newport, Rhode Island, *Mystic Whaler* from Mystic while the *Harvey Gamage* sails out of Northern ports in the summer and then goes to Florida for the winter. The Annapolis-based 90ft *Western Union* also tends to go south for the winter. At New York is the iron schooner *Pioneer*, though strictly speaking she is not in the cruise game but part of South Street Seaport Museum's collection which is on show under the shadow of the highrise buildings of Lower Manhattan. The 57ft *Pioneer* however, is licenced for sail training and passenger work. She also saves the museum a little money by carrying freights such as collecting iron deck beams from Baltimore for the restoration of their Liverpool full rigged ship *Wavertree*. Much of the Pacific coast of America is too open for cruise schooners. When the last San Francisco pilot schooner, the *California*, was sold she became a fishing boat at Newport, Oregon. Had she been on the Atlantic coast she would almost certainly have joined the cruise ship fleet. There was however some interest in restoring the schooner *Thomas F Bayard* at North Vancouver. She had been built in the 1880s for Delaware pilots at Brooklyn and sailed to the Pacific in the Alaska Gold Rush of the 1890s.

The difference between the North American attitude to traditional sailing ships and the European approach is the ease with which replica ships have been accepted in the States. In Europe there has been a great deal of rebuilding old ships while in the United States there has been an avalanche of building brand new replicas. The acceptance of replicas really started with the building of the 112ft schooner *Bluenose II* at Lunenburg, Nova Scotia in 1963. By the late 1970s there were numerous schemes on the Eastern Seaboard of the United States in which new vessels were built on traditional lines. One such enterprise took place at Baltimore, then a run-down city at the top end of Chesapeake Bay. Baltimore was in the process of revitalizing its downtown waterfront area and to encourage local interest it invited the Tall Ships to pay the city a visit during the Bicentennial celebrations of 1976.

From this visit was born the idea of the city building its own ship and they chose one of the famous clipper schooners, known as the Baltimore schooners, as being the most appropriate. The actual vessel, built in public view on the waterfront, was the 90ft *Pride of Baltimore* which was launched with a crane in 1977. To call this ship a replica makes it sound like a plaything, but in fact this is a real sailing ship. The *Pride of Baltimore* logged 30,000 miles sailing in her first two years. Every year since then more ships have been added to the list of new sailers.

At Rockland, Maine, Doug Lee's Yard had rebuilt several 'dude' schooners and then in 1983 they launched a new 90ft wooden, centreboard schooner *Heritage* for the same work. In fact never before in history has there been such a concentrated effort to recreate actual ships from the past. Instead of studying vessels from the past in paintings, it is now possible to go out and learn exactly how they behaved under sail.

CHAPTER 6

Races and rallies

In 1953 it was decided to hold the last Thames Barge Race before this type of working craft finally became extinct. The first major Thames Barge Race had been held in 1863 and was the brainchild of the 'Golden Dustman' Henry Dodd. He had made a fortune from removing refuse off the streets of London and was determined to raise the status of the bargemen by holding an annual 'Sailing Match'. The idea was to encourage good seamanship and to get the crew to keep their barges in good order. This aim was rapidly achieved and competition became so keen that owners started ordering new, faster barges so that the development of the whole type was considerably helped.

There had been local barge races and even, from time to time, private races between barges, but the Thames Match was the prestige event. After World War II barges, converted to yachts, were raced on the River Medway in events organized by the Marine Club at Hoo. The Thames Match was held in 1953 to honour the

The Bahamian trading sloop *Thunder Bird* taking part in the 1965 Out Island Regatta. *Bahamas Tourism*

crowning of Queen Elizabeth II. It was a great nostalgic event with the famous *Sara*, skippered by Jim Uglow, winning the Champion Bowsprit Class. With only thirty-three barges left trading under sail, everyone agreed that such a race would never be held again. In fact the reverse happened; the Grand Coronation Barge Sailing Match proved to be the beginning of a whole new era of highly competitive racing. The revival of the barge races around the Thames estuary is one of the main reasons for the continued existence of the type.

It is a feature of local types of craft that they exist in isolated economic and social pockets dotted around the world. The Bahamas archipelago, which is strung out over the Atlantic from off Florida down towards Haiti, still have many sloops trading under sail. To encourage the maintenance of these sloops the Out Island Regatta, with cash prizes was started in 1954 at George Town, Exuma, roughly in the middle of the Bahamas. These sloops normally take fresh farm products, livestock and seafood from the out islands to Nassau market.

When a hurricane sank about seventy craft at Nassau in 1958, the Out Island Squadron, a group of British, American and Bahamians who ran the Out Island Regatta, raised money to restore the fleet. The qualifications to enter this regatta are that the sloops and schooners must be built of local materials and sailed by a Bahamian crew. Also as a work boat they must in one way or another contribute to support the owner and skipper.

The Bahamian sloops are assumed to have inherited their narrow-headed gaff mainsails from early Dutch craft. In the Netherlands the cargo tjalks still have a sail plan with a narrow headed mainsail and large single headsail. In Freisland, in the north west of The Netherlands local skûtsje, small tjalks, were raced for prizes, usually put up by innkeepers. This began in the middle of the nineteenth century but after World War II there was little commercial use for the steel skûtsje. In order to prevent them from being scrapped, eleven towns and villages bought one each and a series of races started in 1947. These races take place on a different meer each day for a fortnight at the end of August. Over the years the competition to be the champion skûtsje has become extremely fierce. These flat-bottomed barges are sailed very hard in shallow meers and on several occasions they have capsized in strong winds.

During the 1950s well-organized races were starting to stimulate interest in preserving working craft, but another event started an entirely new form of races. In July 1956 sailing ships started to arrive at Dartmouth for a rally before the first International Sail Training Race. The race course was some 780 miles from Torbay to Lisbon and the River Dart was the nearest good anchorage in the west country for a sizable fleet to meet. Ten years before, the Scandinavian sail training ships had all met at Stockholm, but the Dartmouth Rally was the first occasion that a large fleet of sail trainers had ever been assembled.

Dartmouth, clinging to the side of the hill, is a most attractive spot at any time, but with the River Dart lined with square riggers it took on a special magic. The largest training ship was the sixty-year old Portuguese barque *Sagres*, a former cargo ship built as the German full-rigged ship *Rickmer Rickmers*. The Norwegian full rigger *Sørlandet* had not yet been fitted with an engine and had to be towed in and out in the

old way, by a tug.

Nevertheless, this was a very new type of gathering which had been created by a London solicitor, Bernard Morgan, who had no connection with the ships or sailing. Morgan was an idealist who wanted to find a way for young people to get together and foster international friendship. He was convinced of the importance of sail training by Sir William Garthwaite who was so devoted to it that after World War I he bought up square riggers and used his fortune to keep them at sea. Garthwaite's last ship, the four-masted barque *Garthpool*, was lost in 1929 but he still continued to campaign for British sail training ships.

In all, in that first race for sail training ships, vessels from eleven nations took part and the winner and oldest craft in the race was the 103-ton gaff ketch *Moyana*, which had been entered by the School of Navigation, Southampton. When returning to Southampton the *Moyana* was caught in a gale south of the Isles of Scilly. The wind rose so that it was gusting hurricane force and the tremendous seas strained *Moyana*'s hull so that she started making water. A distress call was sent out and when the merchant ship *Clan Maclean* reached her nearly six hours later, her crew of twenty-six were taken off. Later the *Moyana* sank and, although there was no loss of life, this might have been a bad piece of publicity for the new idea of sail training races. In fact, no-one took any notice. The whole idea of square riggers and yachts racing had already caught the public imagination.

The barquentine *Makah* overtaking a scow schooner in the 1884 Master Mariners Regatta, San Francisco. *San Francisco Maritime Museum*

The square topsail cutter *Grönland* and Finkenwerder kutter *Astarte*, a fishing ketch built in 1903, have an informal race on the River Elbe every summer. *Bremerhaven Schiffergilde*

The official title of the race was rather a mouthful so someone dubbed it the "Tall Ships Race". In strict nautical terms a sailing ship can be lofty, but never tall. However the poet John Masefield, who served an apprenticeship on the British four-masted barque *Wanderer*, once used the term 'tall' to refer to a square rigger and no doubt some news editor searching in his mind for a more snappy title was reminded of Masefield's 'Sea Fever'.

The Torbay-Lisbon Tall Ships Race in 1956 was the start of a new era because square riggers were racing for the first time on yachting lines with a handicap system. The first event was organized by the Sail Training International Race Committee which was mainly made up of British Royal Navy officers and ocean racing yachtsmen and had considerable support from all over Europe. Later this committee was remoulded into the Sail Training Association, a permanent body. The STA settled down to organize a Tall Ships Race every other year. Since the original race a whole series of races have been devised throughout the western world, never fixed to one set course, but moved around to different ports.

When the large square-rigged ships gather in any port for Tall Ships Races they attract tens of thousands of spectators. The 1984 Trans-Atlantic Saint Malo-Quebec-Liverpool series of races attracted ships from twenty two nations in which over 3000 young people took part. Sadly the 1984 Tall Ships Race will be remembered for the first tragedy after dozens of races in twenty-eight years. This was the loss of the wooden barque *Marques*, an ex-Spanish coasting schooner, which with forty-one other ships started in the Bermuda-Halifax race on 2 June. Early next morning in heavy weather the *Marques* was about eighty miles off Bermuda when she was hit by a freak squall. She went over, filled and sank in less than a minute. Only nine of the crew were picked up five hours later. The other eighteen which were below or on deck chronically seasick and lashed on with lifelines, went down with the ship. Every ship in the race had to be backed by shore-based administration so the races actively involve several thousand people. There are many volunteer administrators assisting in running these races but this whole international event is administered just by the STA secretary John Hamilton with one full-time and one part-time secretary from an office in Gosport, southern England.

The STA organizes the actual races and advises the ports the ships visit on the ways to handle the problems ashore. The success or failure of the Tall Ships' visit depends largely on the local committees ability. In the early days the costs of administering the races was paid for by private individuals. Now sponsorship from industry has to be sorted out and Cutty Sark Whiskey have footed much of the bill. However the STA have tried to tactfully guide events to keep advertisement and politics out and focus on international friendship. When the American STA was formed they drew on this experience and the motto was 'We will do it like the Brits'.

Since a great many sail training ships are forced to use their engines to keep up with their normal schedules the Tall Ships Races are very important because captains and the ship's company are forced to make the whole passage under sail. That is not to decry the fitting of engines in modern sailing vessels because it is obviously a safety

Terschelling Island pilot boat *Albatros* at Amsterdam Sail, 1980. *Author*

factor in order to be able to manoeuvre clear of a fatal leeshore or a heavily congested area. It is worth remembering that modern sailing ships are only 'sail users', not pure sailing ships like those from the era of deep-water commercial sailing ships.

Large square-rigged ships require a shore-based administration to keep them at sea. This is so expensive and requires so many personnel that it is usually only navies that have the resources to keep a square rigger at sea.

The other part of the traditional ship world, the restored former working craft, is totally different. People who are attracted to beautiful former work boats are often rebelling against any form of authority and are looking for a form of escape from the continual rush from twentieth century life. It is the tremendous rise in wealth in developed western nations since the late 1940s that has made this burst of restoration possible.

Looking back, it is possible to see that in the early 1960s traditional ship races and events were started independently. In the United States Bernard Mackenzie organized a regatta for Friendship sloops at Friendship, Maine in 1961. This lead to the forming of the Friendship Sloop Society to look after the interests of these former lobster boats. The following year the Catboat Association was formed after a rally at Duck Island, off the Connecticut shore of Long Island Sound. The following summer the first antique boat show was held at Clayton, New York and the list of traditional boat events in North America steadily grew. This list includes the starting of a Windjammer Day in New England in 1963 so that all the schooners could meet. On Chesapeake Bay, oystermen were persuaded to take part in annual races. At New York an annual schooner race was started virtually under the shadow of the high rise buildings of Manhattan. Even the famous International Fisherman's Trophy was revived in 1970. True there were no longer any Grand Banker schooners left to fight

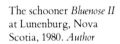

The schooner *Bluenose II* at Lunenburg, Nova Scotia, 1980. *Author*

it out, only yachts, but it was still run on original lines with preliminary eliminating races ending up in the champion American and Nova Scotian schooners meeting in the final battle.

Many new events have been started for traditional boats but in 1965 the San Francisco Master Mariners Regatta was revived. This was begun in 1867 for the Pacific coastal schooners and working boats in the Bay and was held on thirteen occasions until 1891. The biggest turn-out was in 1875 when twenty-three schooners and scows took part. When the race was revived the old practice of each entry being sponsored by a shipping company was repeated. One of the schooners in the first revived race was the *Invader* which held the Honolulu-San Francisco record for a sailing ship of twelve days, fifteen hours.

The gap in time between the two series of San Francisco Master Mariners Regatta,

The bawley *Helen & Violet* racing. The bawleys had loose-footed sails and were used at Harwich, Southend, Leigh, Gravesend, Margate and on the River Medway. *Author*

and the fact that it was successfully restarted shows how deeply rooted traditional sail is a part of any local culture. In Europe many annual races for local work boats were started in Victorian times. These lapsed in the 1920s and were revived in some form in the 1960s.

The work boats with probably the longest run of continual racing are the Essex smacks. The first recorded race for fishing smacks in the River Blackwater was organized by the parson of Bradwell in 1783.

The idea of races had spread from the River Thames, then the centre of British yachting, where the first recorded open cup race was held in 1749. In Victorian times the Thames became polluted and packed with commercial shipping so instead the yachting fraternity used the new-fangled railways to travel to the south coast and made Cowes the yacht racing centre. The fishermen of Essex (like those of the south coast and Falmouth area) spent the winter working on their smacks and the summer as paid hands on the huge yachts. The yachts gave the fishermen a great taste for speed and every autumn, between returning from the yachts and starting fishing, the smacks took part in hard-fought village smack races. The West Mersea Regatta included a race for the oyster smacks right up to World War II. This series was revived again in 1947, but no working smacks took part, only those sailed for pleasure.

The art of sailing a gaff yacht looked like dying out in the post-war years as bermudian sails became the trend on yachts. The possible extinction of gaff yachts was halted by the forming of the Old Gaffers Association in the autumn of 1963 which encouraged racing, restoration and the building of every type of gaff (and lug) working and pleasure craft. As I have entered the East Coast Old Gaffers race for over two decades I have seen how the approach to gaff sails has changed from casual indifference to one of real pride in owning a 'gaffer'. The races have brought topsails back into real use which greatly improves the appearance of a gaff boat and also gives better performance in moderate breezes. The races also improve general seamanship, but the main reason for having them is as a rallying point where gaff sailors can get together. If you have a race however it does breed rivalry.

Although I have always made it a practice to sail on as many different types of traditional craft as possible, to have your own boat, however humble, takes a lot of beating. I deliberately chose a gaff boat as being the most suitable for cruising when I bought the 28ft gaff cutter *Sea Fever*. She was actually a clinker ship's lifeboat with a centreboard added and converted to a yacht. I was immensely fond of *Sea Fever*, but our cruises were done at a very slow speed and in the Gaffers Races we were lucky to even keep the main fleet in sight. I progressed on to the 35ft gaff cutter *L'Atalanta* which was built in Sweden at Landskrona in 1904 as a custom cutter. A boat of this age has to be sailed with some consideration.

Branches of the Old Gaffers Association hold races and rallies all round Britain and the membership of people interested in saving the gaff rig from obscurity is international. Although France and Britain have for centuries disagreed at a political level, there sprung up a wonderful friendship between gaff boat owners on the English south coast and those across the Channel in Brittany in the 1970s. The French gaffers have been obliged to form their own branch – Le Vieux Gréements de France

The spritty barge *Reminder* and Whitstable smack *Rosa & Ada* at the start of the 1979 Colne Race. *Author*

The West Mersea oyster smack *Hyacinth* and Boston smack *Mermaid* in the 1982 Colne Race. Both these smacks had a major rebuild after their working lives ended. The *Hyacinth* is kept in her original state and is sailed without an engine. *Author*

– and pursue their races with cheerful gusto which surprises the English gaffers. In 1982 this new-found interest in traditional craft in Brittany progressed on to another event. This is the Fetes de Pors Beac'h, a huge folk festival which attracts boats from as far away as The Netherlands and Norway.

The idea of races and rallies for gaff-rigged craft seems to have become popular internationally. In Sydney, Australia, gaffers' races have been held every year since

1972 attracting about fifty craft, while on the other side of the continent in Western Australia a separate Old Gaffers Association holds an annual race on the Swan River. One of the larger craft which takes part is the 57ft Thursday Island pearling lugger S'Nicola, built in 1897. The term 'pearling lugger' is a little misleading because this is one of the gaff ketches which was used to collect oyster for its shell. One of the fleets of luggers worked from Thursday Island off the northern tip of Queensland and another worked from Broome, a small very isolated settlement on the Indian Ocean, 2000 miles north of the Swan River at Perth.

The Swan River Old Gaffers Race was started in 1979 by Barry and Doris Hicks who had gone out to Western Australia from Burnham-on-Crouch on the English east coast and although the Hicks loved the beautiful climate of their new land, they sadly missed the smacks and fishing villages of Essex. This is not the only link between the English East Coast and Australia, because in the island of Tasmania one of the local work boat types evolved from the Thames barges. None of these barges ever sailed half way round the world, but settlers in Tasmania built craft between 1800–50 with a flat bottom, leeboards and tiller steered, just like the London river barges. As inter-colonial trade between Tasmania and the neighbouring colonies of Victoria and South Australia increased, a more seaworthy craft was needed to cross the stormy waters of the Bass Strait. The influence of the next stage presumably came from America because fine clipper bows were introduced and the centreboard. The first Hobart ketch to have this improvement is believed to be the 58ft Huon Chief.

The Tasmanian ketches retained the flat bottom and sides and were usually called 'barges'; the Australians quickly started to evolve their own traditional craft by adapting the western hull types to suit local conditions.

The Tasmanian ketches were great sail carriers and set huge jackyard topsails on the main and mizzen. A vast spread of sail allowed the ketches to creep along in light airs, but several were blown straight over when a sudden squall came rushing down a hot valley. The ketch May Queen, which won the last Hobart Ketch Race when it was sailed in 1951, was once capsized by a squall. The first of these annual races had been held in 1848 and these seem to have heightened the Tasmanians' enthusiasm for speed. Certainly the ketches, under their huge spread of canvas, were the main attraction at the Hobart Regatta.

On the other side of Australia right at the end of the working sail era, a short race was started in 1970 for pearling luggers at the Broome Festival of the Pearl. The luggers had evolved from schooners and a reminder of this was that the sail names stayed the same. The main sail was the 'foresail' and the smaller mizzen was the 'mainsail'. The normal working method was to drift sideways with the tide over the ground while the divers on the bottom picked up the shell. Before World War I around 300 luggers operated from Broome, but with the steady decline of the use of oyster shell this dropped to under a dozen motorsailers in the 1970s.

Since time never stands still, traditional boat races keep changing. In England the annual Thames and Medway barge races were revived after the 1953 Grand Coronation Barge Match. For a decade this race achieved the glamour and prestige of the pre-war events with F T Everard & Sons and the London & Rochester Trading

The Essex smack *Iris* in 1979 East Coast Old Gaffers Race with Charles Harker, who rebuilt her, and Yvon le Corre, who sailed her across the Atlantic, on board. Two weeks after this she was totally wrecked on the north east coast of England. The smack did not have an engine and anchored in a calm, but a big swell snapped the chain and drove her on Blackhall beach. *Author*

Company starting to maintain barges just for the two days of racing. The champion racing barges *Sara, Veronica, Sirdar* and *Dreadnought* could be said to have pushed the flat-bottomed spritsail barge to its ultimate limit. The expense of maintaining these over canvased champion class barges finally lead to the two main owners calling a truce and it was agreed in 1963 that the Centenary year should be the last year when the original committee organized the Thames and Medway Matches. These two races were won by Everard's *Veronica* and this company decided to break up this barge as well as the *Sara* and the *Dreadnought*. This decision was hardly surprising as these ageing wooden barges had been 'raced to pieces' under the vast spread of sail. They still went out with a touch of glory for at the end of the 50 mile Thames Race the *Veronica* was timed at 15 knots over the ground when running up to the finish off the 'Ship & Lobster', Gravesend.

In the previous year, 1962, a barge race was revived at Maldon, Essex. Some fifty-three sailing barges were owned in this port in the 1890s and the fastest barges raced annually in the Town Regatta. This was a great local battle between rival skippers which was last raced in 1937 when the *Emma* won. While the barges in the famous Thames & Medway matches had always been given a major and very expensive refit before taking part, the barges for the Maldon and other local races were often just given a bit of a scrub and a fresh coat of paint. This made it possible for every owner to enter.

The race at Maldon was revived because many of the barges now sailed for pleasure were based here and at another similar centre, Pin Mill, a race was also started in 1962. At first the barges taking part in these races had professional bargemen as skippers, but as the years rolled past the number of barges exceeded the number of active skippers. The allowing of barges to be sailed by 'amateur' skippers caused a great row at first, but it was inevitable if barges were going to go on sailing.

As well as Maldon and Pin Mill, other barge races were revived or started at the Medway, Southend, Swale, Thames, Colne and there were short-lived races at Greenwich and Whitstable. The competition created by these races encouraged owners to keep their barges in good order and created an enjoyable reason for keeping barges sailing. Competition to win soon saw some owners fitting better gear and hiring well-known trading skippers as their race skippers. In 1965 Jack Spitty with the *Edith May* was the first man to win all the seasons races, while 'Chubb' Horlock of Mistley with the *May* later dominated the racing scene. In the 1970s a new champion emerged in Alan Reekie of Faversham who sailed his steel charter barge *Ironsides*. No-one seems to even remember the *Ironsides* when she traded under sail, but by fitting a large sail area and cunning racing tactics Alan Reekie made her virtually unbeatable and won all the races in 1982. He gave up racing the following year because he had 'done it all'. It had been Alan's love for 'improving' barge gear that led to the introduction of large steel leeboards in 1980.

In recent decades, although about fifty spritsail barges are in sailing order, most of them are fitted with engines. The last long passage made by sailing barge without an engine was in 1966 when the *Venta* was sailed from Stockholm back to Maldon by John Fairbrother. In the Baltic, under the shelter of Fehmarn Island, the *Venta* averaged 9½ knots for several hours in a strong breeze. The North Sea crossing of 274 miles was done at an average of 5½ knots.

Among the charter barges one skipper owner has resisted the temptation of fitting an engine and continuing to operate under sail only. This is Peter Dodds with the *Mirosa* which, although based at Faversham, has sailed during the summer anywhere between the River Humber and Cowes. In the races the beautifully-shaped *Mirosa* has always been amongst the prize winners. She is also a very handy barge, but the world has changed since she was built by Howard at Maldon in 1892 as a 'stackie' to carry hay and straw from Essex to feed the horses then used on the streets of London. Container ships and european ferries must be added to all the age-old dangers of the sea. These are capable of over twenty knots while a sailing barge has only the fickle power of the wind to keep clear of such modern monsters.

While all the day barge races with cheerful prizegivings ashore are good fun, perhaps the most important is the sixty-mile Gravesend to Pin Mill Challenge Match because it keeps alive the art of passage making under sail. Since it was started in 1978 the only true drama in this race was in 1981 when *Vigilant*, skippered by Mike Lungley was beating into Harwich Harbour in a fresh breeze when the stemhead band parted and the mast crashed down on the deck. Barge masts are stepped in a case so that they could be lowered to go under bridges in the trading days. The *Vigilant's* mainmast, topmast and half a ton of steel sprit and a mass of sails fell down on the deck, but fortunately no one was injured.

The 1982 passage race was won by *Ironsides* which is only a stemhead staysail barge.

The skipper Jim Stone of Mistley and his victorious race crew on the new steel barge *Reminder* in 1929. *Harold Horlock*

Skipper Alan Reekie has strong views that a bowsprit is unnecessary on a barge. However the coasting barges always had a bowsprit and the next barge to finish was the bowsprit barge *Mirosa*.

After this race seventeen barges went up the River Orwell to attend the Maritime Ipswich Rally at Ipswich. This was one of a series of events held in 1982 which was part of Britain's Maritime Heritage Year. At Ipswich there was a strong emphasis on starting a local sail training scheme and on drawing attention to the historic Wet Dock so that a new use could be found for it when commercial traffic ceased. Traditional craft are often used to help in the plight of saving historic waterside buildings which at Ipswich includes a Tudor merchant's house and warehouse and a Victorian Customs House.

Ipswich is one of those places which can be described as a 'sailing ship port' because there is nearly always some form of traditional vessel there. Ipswich's claim to this proud title is kept by sailing barges being based there, but in 1981 the square rigger connection was renewed by the Norwegian full-rigged ship *Sørlandet* which called in for supplies while on passage from New York to Kristiansand. This was the first square rigger to visit the port since the four-masted barque *Abraham Rydberg* arrived from Australia with grain in 1939.

Some places just seem to attract sailing vessels. On the English east coast it is Ipswich, Pin Mill, Brightlingsea, Maldon, Faversham and St Katharine's Dock, London. The final event of each year in this area in which most of the local craft enter is the Colne Smack and Sailing Barge Match held in September off Brightlingsea. The original race was held until 1922 and then in 1971 it was revived. Local enthusiasts formed the Colne Smack Preservation Society which has leased part of Aldous Yard where many of the surviving were built so that the smacks and bawleys could be kept in their home waters. This society has not yet restored the smack dock, but the idea of preserving a waterside area as well as local craft seems appropriate.

On the east coast it is mostly local craft which have been rigged out after their trading or fishing careers have finished. For instance the huge steel coasting sailing barge *Will*, ex-*Will Everard*, goes on promotion voyages for her owners OCL Containers, while the *Xylonite* is a charter barge. Two brothers, Robin and Anthony Davies, have used Brightlingsea and the convenient Pyefleet anchorage across the River Colne as a base for rigging out wooden Danish traders. So far this has culminated into owning the brigantine *Soren Larsen* and managing the Guernsey-registered barque *Kaskelot* in charter work, mostly for films.

There is so much activity restoring traditional craft and reviving races in some areas that it is easy to forget that other places have been left untouched by this activity. In the Channel Islands in the 1880s over 700 fishing vessels, all sail, were registered at Guernsey and Jersey. It is hardly surprising in an age when so many people made their entertainment out of their work that work boat races were popular on Guernsey.

The main Guernsey race was at St Peter's Port. These were being held in the 1880s and lasted until 1950. The villages of Sampson's and Grande Havre had regattas and a regatta was also started in 1910 at Rocquaire Bay, which is open to the Atlantic. The fishing boats were kept in sheltered inlets around Rocquaire Bay and from here the 40ft three-masted mackerel boats went out to the open sea and to the Casquets. The introduction of engines made it more feasible to operate from St Peter's Port so that there were no three masters at Rocquaire Bay after 1914. However, the inshore fishing boats raced here from 1920–28 and then the regatta lapsed until 1971. After this only yachts came, although the Old Gaffers from the South Coast of England gave the regatta colour for a few years, but Guernsey's sailing fishing fleet is now just a folk memory.

Since traditional craft are undoubtedly beautiful to look at and enjoyable to sail on we are improving the environment by keeping them sailing. We are saving the best pieces of the past while, hopefully eliminating the hardships and poverty that sometimes went with them. Certainly by continuing to sail these craft we learn more about the past and in consequence understand our destiny.

In practice, one boat sailing on its own has a struggle to keep alive a local tradition, but if a fleet of boats can be kept sailing then the whole social culture continues to revolve around them, just as it did when they were working. This process of putting the clock back has been going on since the 1960s and there has been a steady increase in the number of traditional craft with many extinct boat types reappearing. Provided hulls continue to be rebuilt and replaced, this process will continue. Traditional craft have survived the transition into our age of technology and will go on sailing into the future.

The Polish barquentine
Pogoria leaving Falmouth
at the start of the 1982
Tall Ships Race to Lisbon.
Falmouth Packet

Traditional craft lists

The following gazetteer is intended as an aid to identifying some of the traditional vessels which might be seen sailing. Many other traditional vessels are on display individually or in museums, but these are not included as information is usually available with the vessel. Changes to this list are happening all the time as traditional ships and smaller craft are abandoned or broken up.

Much of the information here has been gathered for the 'Sail Review' column for *Sea Breezes* which I have been compiling for the past eighteen years and has usually been supplied by owners, captains and crews of vessels concerned. This does not guarantee accuracy but they are usually the most reliable source. In the case of small craft it is now very difficult to be absolutely accurate about their early history.

In the 1960s a group of readers of 'Sail Review' formed Mariners International, a group which was devoted to getting their members to sea in sail and Erik Abranson edited *Notice to Mariners* which became *Windjammer* when they reformed as Mariners

The German barque Passat, built in 1911, made her last voyage under sail in 1957 and even after over a quarter of a century as a stationary training ship still looks in good order. She is seen here at Lübeck right on West Germany's border with East Germany. Author

The Norfolk Rivers cruisers *Goldfish* and *Melody* tacking through Reedham's opened railway bridge show how highly manoeuvrable these inland waterways craft are. These yachts can turn virtually in their own length. *Author*

International Club. Additional facts have been gleaned from Rick Hogben's column in *Ships Monthly* and the magazine *Traditional Sail Review*. In North America the *Wooden Boat* is highly informative on the technical and historical side of traditional craft, while the National Maritime Historical Society and World Ship Trust jointly produce *Sea History*, edited by Peter Stanford with the help of Ted Miles and from information supplied by Norman Brouwer, curator of ships at the South Street Seaport Museum, New York.

Many of the organizations devoted to preserving and holding races for traditional ships also publish their own newsletters which often supply histories. Particularly good news magazines are published by Traeskibs Sammenslutningen (Danish Wooden Ship Society), the Sveriges Sgelfartygs (Swedish Traditional Ship Association) and the German Der Freunde Des Gaffelriggs (Friends of the Gaff Rig).

All vessels are wooden-built unless otherwise specified. The numbers in brackets refer to page numbers and those in italics to illustrations.

The Weiringeraaks *WR 54* and *WR 17*, Zuiderzee fishing craft from Weiringen, at the Amsterdam Sail 1980. *Author*

Four Masted Barques

Kaiwo Maru (steel) (42)
A 4343-ton displacement sister ship to
Nippon Maru built at Kawasaki Yard,
Kobe, Hondo in 1930. This Japanese
training ship normally carries 27
officers, 48 crew and 120 cadets. She
spent World War II as a motor ship and
was returned to sail in 1954. Ships of the
Japanese merchant navy have the suffix
Maru meaning 'sea', thus 'Kaiwo Maru'
means 'sea king'. Her home port is
Tokyo.

Kruzenstern (steel) (43, 44, *134*)
This 3100 gross ton barque was built in
1926 by J C Tecklenborg for L Laeisz of
Hamburg as the *Padua*. She was the last
of the famous Flying P Line to be built
and also the last four-masted cargo-
carrying barque to be built. She was
built with accommodation for 40 cadets
and was a cargo-carrying cadet ship in
the nitrate trade. In 1930 she lost four
men overboard while rounding Cape
Horn. The Laeisz captains were under
instruction to make fast passages and
discipline aboard the Flying P ships was
very strict. In 1932 the last two Laeisz
sailers, *Padua* and *Priwall*, were laid up
because of a slump in freights to South
America. The German Government
helped to pay for her to go to sea again
and she completed her record passage of
67 days from Hamburg-Port Lincoln,
South Australia in 1934 and then came
back to Queenstown (Cobh) in 100 days
with grain for Barry. In her last voyage
under the German flag she was 93 days
from Port Lincoln to Fastnet with grain
for Glasgow.

When World War II started, *Padua* was
back at Hamburg, but at the end of the
war she was laid up at Flensburg. In
1946 she was handed over to Russia and
eventually she went back to sea as a
training ship, renamed *Kruzenstern*, after
an explorer. She appears to be based at
the Baltic port of Riga and is a training
ship for young people going into the

Russian fishing fleet. In 1974 the
Kruzenstern and the barque *Tovaristsch*
were the first Russian ships to enter the
Tall Ships Races. Her home port is
Riga.

Nippon Maru (steel) (42)
Nippon means Japan, and this barque is
the sister ship of *Kaiwo Maru* built by
Kawasaki Yard in 1930 to train officers
in the merchant navy. All the rigging
and sails were supplied by Ramage &
Ferguson, Leith. The sails are smaller
than those used on a European barque
because the Japanese are smaller people.
To accommodate a large number of
cadets she has high sides and her
appearance is further spoilt by a funnel
between the main and mizzen masts.
During World War II she had all the
yards removed and she operated as a
motor vessel. She was rigged out again
in 1952 and makes regular long training
voyages in the Pacific. In 1961 she
crossed the Pacific in 17½ days beating
her sister ship by 34 hours in the first
Pacific sail training race.

Nippon Maru II (steel)
Built by Sumitomo Heavy Industries,
Tokyo in 1984 to replace the 1930
Nippon Maru. The first four-masted
barque built for over fifty years, she is
4500 tons and has a total crew of 190.
Her home port is Tokyo. The 1930
Kaiwo Maru was also due to be replaced.

Sea Cloud of Grand Cayman (steel) (*55, 131*)
The largest yacht ever built, she was
built by Germania Werft, Kiel,
Germany in 1930 for the American
millionairess Mrs Marjorie Hutton Post.
Originally named the *Hussar II*, she was
316ft long and 2323 gross tons. Later she
belonged to the US Ambassador to
Russia who used her as a floating palace
at Leningrad. She spent World War II
as a US patrol ship and then became the
Angelita, owned by the President of the
Dominican Republic. In 1963 she was
laid up at Panama under the name *Patria*.

She appears to have changed hands several times and in 1968 was in Naples. In 1979, under German ownership and the flag of Grand Cayman Islands in the West Indies, she became a cruise ship with a crew of around fifty-five. Her home port is Hamburg.

Sedov (steel) (*33*, 43, 44)
At 5300 tons displacement, the world's largest active sailing ship. She was built by Germania Werft, Kiel in 1921 for F A Vinnen of Bremen, Germany as the *Magdalene Vinnen*. She was fitted with a small diesel auxiliary engine when launched and had accommodation for cadets. She was originally in the nitrate trade from Chile round Cape Horn to Germany, although by the 1930s she had moved to the Australia grain trade. At the start of this period another four-masted barque had the same name, but was sailing under the Italian flag; this vessel had been the *Dunstaffnage* but was scrapped in the 1920s.

In 1936 the *Magdalene Vinnen* was sold to the Norddeutsche Lloyd of Bremen, became *Kommodore Johnsen* and remained in the Australian trade. She was nearly lost in 1937 on a voyage from Buenos Aires to Hamburg, when the bulk cargo shifted and she listed to 55°. The abnormally large ship's crew (72, against the usual 30) shifted the grain back and

thus the ship was saved. During World War II this barque was based at Flensburg and made short training voyages in the Baltic. After the war she was laid up at Hamburg and was then moved to Kiel where she was taken over by Russia and towed away in 1950. She was renamed *Sedov* after a Russian polar explorer in the 1950s and in the early 1960s was seen passing through the Baltic on training voyages. She appears to have been laid up for most of the 1970s but in 1981 was at sea again and in 1982 visited the Parade of Sail for sail training ships at Lisbon. She also visited Hamburg where many of her former German crew members were entertained aboard.

Adventure sailing in millionaire style: the four-masted barque *Sea Cloud* now sailing as a cruise ship, operating from Hamburg.

Barques

Cuauhtémoc (steel) (43)
Built at Celaya Shipyard, Bilbao, Spain, for the Mexican Navy, and named after the last Aztec emperor. At 220ft long, she is slightly larger than the other Senermar-designed barques from the Bilbao yard. She sets a royal and single topgallant sails over double topsails, and carries a crew of 180 of which 95 are permanent. Her home port is Acapulco.

Eagle (steel) (39, 109)
Built in 1936 by Blohm & Voss, Hamburg, as the German training ship *Horst Wessel* but only made a few training voyages. She is slightly larger

than her predecessor *Gorch Fock I*, now the Russian *Tovaristsch*. In 1946 the *Horst Wessel* was handed over to the United States at Bremerhaven, and she became the US Coast Guard training ship *Eagle* based at New London, Connecticut. Every summer she sails to Europe or Central America, usually accompanied by US Coast Guard motorships and cadets change ships during the voyage. Occasionally she takes part in Tall Ship Races. The *Eagle* was the host ship which led fifteen large sailing ships and over 100 small training vessels in Operation Sail's parade up New York harbour on 4 July 1976. There were over 300 vessels officially entered for this parade.

Elissa (steel) (94)

Built by Alexander Hall of Aberdeen, Scotland in 1877 for Henry F Watt of Liverpool. She traded to South America, Canada, India, Burma and Australia etc, and in 1897 was sold to Norwegian owners Bugge & Olsen who kept her for fourteen years; she then became a barquentine, *Gustaf*, under Swedish ownership, in 1930 a motor schooner under Finnish owners, then a motor ship. Sold to Greek owners in 1960, she became *Achaios* and then *Pioneer*. She ended the 1960s being used to smuggle cigarettes from Yugoslavia to Italy. Purchased by Peter Throckmorton for preservation, she was bought in 1975 by the Galveston Historical Foundation. In 1977 a quarter of the hull was renewed at Piraeus, Greece, and in 1979 she was towed to Galveston where the rebuilding continued. In 1982 she went out for her first sail completely restored as a sailing museum ship. Her home port is Galveston.

Gloria (steel) (43)

This 1300-ton 250ft barque was built at Bilbao, Spain, in 1968 for the Colombian Navy. She is run by the Armada Nacional de Colombia with a total crew of 145 of which 9 are officers, 5 officers instructors, 80 cadets, 30 petty officers, 12 sailors and 9 auxiliary personnel. Her sail area is 15,050 sq ft and the design was tested in the wind tunnel of the National Institute of Technical Aeronautics in Madrid.

Golden Hinde

Replica of Sir Francis Drake's Elizabethan galley built by J Hinks & Son, Appledore in 1973 for the Golden Hind Corporation of San Francisco. After launching, she sailed out to San Francisco where she was opened to the public. Later she was sailed by Captain Adrian Small of Brixham to Japan for use in a film, *Shogun*, and then returned to England where she was opened to the public at ports on the south coast of

England, including Poole. She later was moved to Scotland and in 1984 was up for sale.

Gorch Fock II (steel) (36, 39)

Built by Blohm & Voss in 1958 as a training ship for the German Federal Navy, one of several training ships built by them. At 266ft, she is 26ft longer than the four barques built by Blohm & Voss between 1933–37. This 1760-tons displacement barque has the usual German double spanker gaffs on the mizzen so that the sails can be brailed in. 'Gorch Fock' is the pen name of the German nautical writer Hans Kinau who was drowned in the Skagerrak in 1916. The barque is based at Kiel, usually making two short voyages into the North Sea and one long Atlantic voyage in a year. A frequent entrant in the Tall Ships Races, in 1968 she was six and a half days sailing round the course from Gothenburg to Fair Isle and back to Kristiansand. This made her the winner, beating *Sørlandet* which took eight days and the *Christian Radich* which took sixteen days. Her home port is Kiel.

Guayas (steel) (43)

Built at Bilbao, in 1977 as a training ship for Ecuador. In 1980 she was the only square rigger to take part in all the Tall Ships Races and cruises from Cartagena, Colombia, to Norfolk, Virginia, then Boston, Massachusetts and across the Atlantic to Kristiansand, Norway. From here she went on to Karlskrona, Sweden and finally to Amsterdam. These races are often cancelled in the middle because the ships have to keep to the schedule of events organized ashore. Her home port is Guayaquil.

Kaskelot (105, 126)

Built in 1947 as a 120ft motor ship by Ring Andersen, Svendborg, for the Royal Danish Greenland Company to operate in Greenland, including carrying a doctor aboard. She worked in the Faeroes after 1972, but in the autumn of 1983 was sold at Frederikshavn as the *Ane Marie Greneus*. Bought by

Clearwater Holdings of Jersey and managed by Robin Davies of Square Sail, she was converted at Jacobsens Plads, Troense, to the barque *Kaskelot* for chartering to film companies. She sailed to Greenland in 1984 to take the role of the *Terra Nova*.

La Dame de Serk (composite)
Built by Dubigeon in 1955 as a cruiser sterned training ship for the French Navy. Sold in about 1962 to commercial owners and then in 1969 to the Sark Shipping Company. Laid up in London for a long period and then converted to a barque with painted gunports. Started sailing in 1984 with sails on the mizzen and foremast.

Merkur
Built as a fishing vessel at Skedervik, Sweden in 1970 on Canadian fishing boat lines. The Canadians who ordered the vessel never took delivery and instead she was sold to Esbjerg as a trawler. She was bought in 1981 by David Summerskill to replace the brigantine *Luna*, wrecked at Great Yarmouth; she was rigged out lightly as a barque, but by 1983 all passages had been made under power.

Mircea (steel) (39)
Built by Blohm & Voss in 1938 for Romania and named after the fourteenth century Prince Mircea of Romania. In 1939 she sailed to Constanta on the Black Sea and made one short Mediterranean voyage before World War II. During the war she was seized by Russia, but later handed back to Romania. In 1966 she had a refit and a new 1000 hp engine was fitted at Hamburg. When bound back to the Black Sea she met bad weather in the English Channel and put into the Solent for shelter. At that time she had a crew of 100 and normally made month-long training voyages. Her home port is Constanta on the Black Sea.

Sagres II (steel) (39, 42)
Built by Blohm & Voss in 1937 as the 1869 displacement tons German naval training ship *Albert Leo Schlageter*. She made a few voyages before being

damaged by mines in World War II. She was handed over, damaged, to the USA who had no use for her, so in 1948 she became the Brazilian training ship *Guanabara*. In 1961 she was sold to the Portuguese Navy to replace *Sagres I*, ex-*Rickmer Rickmers*. The *Sagres II* sailed round the world in 1979 via Panama and Suez canals. Her home port is Lisbon.

Simon Bolivar (steel) (43)
Built at Celaya shipyard, Bilbao, Spain in 1980 for the Venezuelan navy. Has a total crew of 181.

Star of India (iron)
The barque *Star of India* was built at Ramsey, Isle of Man in 1863 as the 1197 gross ton full-rigged ship *Euterpe*. First owned in Liverpool, she traded to Calcutta and then spent twenty-seven years, under the ownership of Shaw, Savill & Albion, trading from Britain to South Australia and New Zealand. In 1899 she was sold to a San Francisco owner and under the Hawaiian flag carried timber from Puget Sound to Australia. Then in 1901 she joined the Alaska Packer Association fleet as the barque *Star of India*. In 1926 she was laid up and was in a bad state by 1959 when a group from San Diego had her restored as a museum ship for her centenary year. The *Star of India* just qualifies as an active ship because in 1976, the Bicentennial year, she was taken out for a sail. Her home port is San Diego.

Statsraad Lehmkuhl (steel) (40)
Built as the 1701 gross ton German sail training ship *Grossherzog Friedrich August* at Bremerhaven in 1914. Due to World War I she never made a voyage under the German flag and was eventually handed over to Britain as part of war reparations. The British Government gave her to Newcastle shipowners who had no use for her so they sold her in 1922 to the Norwegian Bergen Steamship Company who formed an association to run her as a training ship under the name *Statsraad Lehmkuhl*. Until 1939 she made regular voyages as a training ship. Throughout World War II she was used by German

troops as a depot ship and went back to sea as a training ship in 1946. She took part in the 1960 Ostend-Oslo Tall Ships Race, but in the 1960s, due to the cost of maintaining an ageing ship, she gradually reduced her number of sea voyages. She came third in the 1970 Plymouth-Tenerife Tall Ships Race with 96 cadets aboard and in the late 1970s the city of Bergen took

on part ownership and planned to get her back to sea.

Tovaristsch (steel) (*35*, 43, 44)
Built by Blohm & Voss in 1933 as the German Navy training barque *Gorch Fock*. Became the Russian *Tovaristsch* in 1948. Not known whether she was still going to sea in 1984.

Full Rigged Ships

The Russian four-masted barque *Kruzenstern* and the Norwegian full-rigged ship *Christian Radich* leaving Plymouth at the start of the Tall Ships Race to the New York Operation Sail in 1976. *Author*

Amerigo Vespucci (steel) (*36*)
In the inter-war years the Italian Navy had two training ships built at Castellamare di Stabia on the lines of an early nineteenth century British man of war, but larger. One ship was the *Cristoforo Colombo*, built in 1928, which was handed over to Russia after World War II and was renamed *Dunay* (Danube) but she has not been seen at sea for a long time. The other, the *Amerigo Vespucci*, built in 1930 for the Naval Academy at Livorno, has been used for training officers for the Italian Navy. *Amerigo Vespucci* has made many long voyages, but because of her high superstructure is rather a poor sailer and normally attends the sail parades at the beginning or end of the Talls Ships Races rather than taking part. Her home port is La Spezia.

Christian Radich (steel) (40, 42, *134*)
Built at Sandefjord as a training ship for Ostlandets Skoleskib, the Merchant Navy organization of Oslo, in 1937. At only 207 tons net, she is quite small for a full rigged

ship. She made two long voyages and was then caught up in New York when World War II started. While the *Danmark* stayed in New York, the *Christian Radich* returned to Norway and was later seized at Horten by German troops. She ended up as a bare hull, partly sunk, at Flensburg at the end of the war, but was taken back to Sandefjord for a major refit and began sailing again in 1947. She usually makes one long voyage across the Atlantic every year. *Christian Radich* took part in the first Tall Ships Race and has entered regularly since then. Her home port is Oslo.

Danmark (steel) (40)
Built in 1932 at Nakskov, Denmark as a training ship for the Danish merchant navy, and owned by the Ministry of Shipping and based at Copenhagen. She was visiting the World Fair at New York when World War II started, and the Danish Government ordered the captain of the ship, which carried 120 cadets, to hand her over to the US Government. She was moved to Jacksonville, Florida and later became a training ship for the US Coast Guard at New London, Connecticut. After the war, the *Danmark* sailed for home and the USCG decided to continue with sail training and acquired the German *Horst Wessel* which was renamed *Eagle*. The *Danmark* still makes long training voyages under the Danish flag and takes part in the Tall Ships Races. She is based in Copenhagen.

Dar Mlodziezy (steel) (*44*, *135*)
Built at Gdansk, Poland, in 1981 to replace the Polish merchant navy training ship *Dar Pomorza* which was then seventy-

two years old and had become a museum ship. 'Dar Mlodziezy' means 'Youth's Gift'. She has a displacement tonnage of 2950 and has 2936 sq m sail. There is a crew of 196 which includes a permanent crew of 38 officers and men. Her first voyage in 1982 included taking part in the Falmouth-Lisbon Tall Ships Races. Her home port is Gdansk.

Georg Stage (steel) (*35*, 40)
Built at Frederikshavn, Denmark, in 1935 for Georg Stage Minde (Georg Stage Memorial Foundation) of Copenhagen to replace another *Georg Stage* built in 1882. At only 134ft and 298 gross tons she is really too small to be a full rigged ship, but provides plenty of work for her large crew of over eighty. She is primarily used for training boys for the merchant service, although about thirty leave each autumn to join the *Danmark*. The ship is laid up in the winter and normally in the early summer makes a Baltic cruise before making longer voyages into the North Sea. In 1956 she finished 12th in the Torbay-Lisbon Tall Ships Race, but was caught in a Force 10 coming back across the Bay of Biscay and at one stage was in danger of being driven ashore. Since then she has only taken part in the races in her normal cruising limits. One of her furthest voyages was from Copenhagen, her home port, to St Peter's Port, Guernsey in 1983.

HMS *Bounty* (steel sheathed in wood above the waterline)
Built in 1978 at Whangarey Engineering Co, Whangarey, New Zealand, for a film on Captain Bligh and the 1789 mutiny of the *Bounty*. The sea trials took place in 1979 in Bream Bay with the crew from the New Zealand sail training schooner *Spirit of Adventure*, but the film of this ship was commissioned but never made. In 1981 the *Bounty* was sailed again for Prince Charles' visit to New Zealand. Another *Bounty* replica, built of wood by Smith & Rhuland, Lunenburg, Nova Scotia in 1960, is a museum ship. Both replicas are larger than the original *Bounty*, and both are based at St Petersburg, Forida.

HMS *Rose*
Built by Smith & Rhuland, Lunenburg, Nova Scotia, in 1970 as a replica of the 450-ton HMS *Rose* built in 1756 which had spent much of her active life on the eastern seaboard of America. The West India Packet Company, Newport, Rhode Island, has operated this replica. Her home port is Newport.

Libertad (steel) (42, 44)
Built at the Argentinian State Shipyard, Rio Santiago, in 1962 for the Argentine Navy. She was at that time the world's largest active sailing vessel – length 300ft, 3720 displacement tons and a total crew of 383. Every year she makes a cruise along the South American coast to visit ports in North America and then across to northern Europe before returning to Buenos Aires. She crossed the Atlantic from Halifax, Nova Scotia, to Bull Rock lighthouse on the southern coast of Ireland in 1966 in 6 days 21 hours. For much of this record passage she was sailing at 12 knots in Force 8–9. On one day when Rear Admiral (R) Ricardo Franke increased sail in a Force 9, the *Libertad* reached 16.5 knots and sailed 272.8 miles. Her home port is Buenos Aires.

Sørlandet (steel) (40, 125)
This Norwegian 640-ton sail training ship was built at Kristiansand in 1927. This 186ft merchant navy training ship was built with money given by a shipowner

The Polish youth training full rigged ship *Dar Mlodziezy* leaving St Malo for the 1984 Tall Ships Races to Quebec City, Canada. *Author*

who stipulated that the ship must be a pure sailing ship. Seized by the Nazis in World War II and eventually sunk by Russians in air attacks on Kirkenes, beyond the Arctic Circle, she was raised and returned to service in 1948 and, before being fitted with an engine in 1960, was the last pure sail training ship. In the 1966 Falmouth-Skaw Tall Ships Race *Sørlandet* came first, followed by *Christian Radich*, *Statsraad Lehmkuhl*, *Danmark* and *Georg Stage*. She entered the Tall Ships races regularly at that time, but in 1972 was replaced by the motor ship *Sjøkurs*, and was laid up at Kristiansand. Later she was presented to the town. After a major refit she was back to sea in 1980 as a charter training ship. Her home port is Kristiansand.

Barquentines

The *Regina Maris* setting an excessive amount of sail for the benefit of the camera, off the Florida coast. *J & S Wilson*

Amorina (steel)
A Swedish lightship built at Gothenburg in 1934. She was on station at N Strömgrönd and Sydostbrojtan LV, and was later bought by the Swedish Square Sail Training Society who had previously had the ageing wooden jackass barque *Meta ar Bixelkrok* in the Mediterranean. In 1980 the *Amorina* was converted to a barquentine at Monica Yard, Aveiro, Portugal.

Barbra Negro
Built for whale catching in Norway in 1896. She was bought by German-Canadian Albert Spidl and converted to a barquentine with a galleon stern with windows. Sailed in 1974 for New York from Portsmouth and was then based on Long Island Sound.

Dewarutji (steel)
This 886-tons displacement barquentine was built at H C Stulcken & Son, Hamburg, in 1953 as a sail training vessel for the Indonesian Navy.

Elizabeth Smit
A minesweeper built for the Royal Navy by Herd & McKenzie of Buckie, Scotland in 1940. She was handed over to the Royal Netherlands Navy as *Marken* and then became a Scout Training Ship. She was later bought by Harry Smit and converted to a barquentine at Muiden on the Ijsselmeer; Currently she is the largest Dutch charter ship and operates from Amsterdam.

Gazela Primeiro
Built at Cacilhas, Portugal in 1883, and rebuilt at Setubal in 1900. Thereafter she sailed every summer to the Grand Banks with thirty dories for cod fishing. In 1931 she made her first fishing voyage to the Greenland Fishery, and, when she was finally laid up near Lisbon in the late 1960s, she was the last commercial square rigger. She was presented to the Philadelphia Maritime Museum and in 1971 sailed across the Atlantic; after this she was then given a major refit. In 1976 she was involved in a collision with the *Mircea* and the barquentine *Erawan* at the start of the Bermuda-Newport Tall Ships Race, but she was repaired at Mystic in time for the New York Parade of Sail. Plans to use her as a sail training ship were halted in 1979 because she had not been built in the United States. She subsequently became a Museum Ship at Penn's Landing, Philadelphia, and in 1984 was being fitted out to sail to Quebec City Tall Ships Rally.

Iskra (II) steel
Built at Gdansk, Poland in 1982 as a Polish Navy training ship and a near sister ship to *Pogoria*.

Kaliakra steel
Built at Gdansk, Poland in 1984 as a
Bulgarian training ship. A near sister ship
to *Pogoria*.

Onaygorah (reinforced concrete)
A vessel built at Montreal in 1919 as a
war-time experiment. She was the
Canadian Coast Guard buoy and
lighthouse tender *Concretia* until sinking
off Kingston, Ontario, in 1930. She was
raised in 1979 and rigged out as a
barquentine but has masts so that she
could eventually become a barque. She
sailed for the Pacific in 1982 to do marine
research.

Our Svanen
Built in Denmark as a typical jacht Baltic
trader in 1922. Her Danish name was
Svanen, but the 'Our' was added when she
was registered at Stornoway in the
Hebrides after being rigged out at Poole
in 1978 to distinguish her from another
Danish *Svanen*. Owned by Doug and
Margaret Havers and based at Victoria,
British Columbia, she has been making
sail training voyages in the Pacific.

Palinuro (steel)
Built in 1935 at Nantes as the 858 gross ton
Commandant Louis Richard in a final attempt
by France to keep sailing vessels in the
Grand Bank dory fishing fleet. She still
went, as a motor ship, to the Grand Banks
from Brittany after World War II, but

was sold in 1955 to the Italian Navy and
converted to a barquentine for training.
Her home port is La Maddelena.

Pogoria (steel) (*127*)
Modern steel-hulled vessel with a flat
transom stern built for sail training at
Gdansk, Poland in 1980. She is 47m by 8m
by 3.5m and has a 310 hp diesel engine. She
is owned by Iron Shackle Fraternity whose
Four Shackle emblem is carried on her
square sail. Her home port is Gdansk.

Regina Maris (*48*, 49, 50, 51–5, 64, *136*)
Built by Ring Andersen, Svendborg as a
114ft three-masted schooner in 1908 for
Swedish owners in Raa. She traded mostly
in European waters and was fitted with
her first auxiliary engine in 1931. Badly
damaged by fire in 1964, she was sold to
John and Sigfried Wilson, Arendal, Norway,
where she was totally rebuilt as a barquentine and, because of her age, placed under
the Maltese flag. She made several long adventure voyages including one round-the-
world voyage. In 1973 at Ensenada, Mexico
she was sold to British owners and returned
to Southampton. She later made a voyage to
South America, was sold in Greece in 1976 to
Ocean Research & Education of Boston,
Massachusetts. She is currently used for
studying whales around Greenland in the
summer and goes to the West Indies in the
winter.

The brig *Ciudad De Inca*
under power in the River
Orwell, 1982. *Author*

Brigs

Cuidad De Inca (*41*, 65, *137*)
Built at Ibiza in 1856. She traded to Cuba
taking gold bullion out and returning to
Spain with tobacco. She was bought
derelict by Robin Cecil Wright and Mark
Litchfield in 1980, rebuilt at Barbate de
Franco and rigged out as a brig for film work
work which did not materialize. She sailed
to England in 1982 and made a clockwise
voyage round Britain in the Clipper
Challenge, a series of port-to-port races
with the *Marques*, which was organized by
the China Clipper Society. The *Inca* is one of
the few square riggers to use studding sails.
In the autumn of 1983 she sailed for the
West Indies and on to the United States.

The British brig *Royalist* at the start of the 1982 Falmouth-Lisbon Tall Ships Race. The run before the wind suited *Royalist* and she was the overall winner. *Falmouth Packet*

Pilgrim

Built by A Neilsen, Denmark in 1945 as the motor schooner *Joal*. She was converted in Portugal to a brig and given the name *Pilgrim* after the brig that the author Richard Henry Dana sailed on in the 1850s. In 1984 she was at the Nautical Heritage Museum at Dana Point, California. Her home port is Los Angeles.

Pilgrim of Newport

A 97ft brig built on Baltimore clipper lines in southern California. Technically a snow, a brig with a gaff mizzen on a pole immediately aft of the mizzen mast, she was built by Dennis Holland over a period of fourteen years. Her home port is Los Angeles.

Royalist (steel) (46, 58, *138*)

Built at Cowes, Isle of Wight, in 1971 for the Sea Cadet Corps and based at Portsmouth. Designed by Colin Mudie, this 76ft sail training vessel normally makes weekly cruises with a crew of 28.

Unicorn

Built at Sibbo, Finland in 1948 as a galease. She traded with gravel between Borgaa and Helsingfors until bought in 1971 by three Americans and a Swede. She was converted at Ystad, Sweden to an 1870s-style brig, and in 1973 arrived at New York. Next she became a training ship in Florida and in 1982 was undertaking charter work from St Lucia in the West Indies.

Varuna

A 93ft sail training brig built at Alcock, Ashdown, Bhavanger, India, in 1979 and commissioned at Bombay for India's Sea Cadet Corps. A sister ship to the British brig *Royalist*.

Brigantines

Asgard A Do

Built in 1981 by John Tyrell & Sons, Arklow, Ireland as an 85ft training ship. Her name means *Asgard II* in Gaelic, by which name she is more generally known. This vessel took the place of a ketch of the same name built in Norway in 1905 for Erskine Childers, which was used as a training ship between 1961–74.

Black Pearl

Built as a yacht in 1948 at Wickford, Rhode Island. She was bought in 1959 by Barclay Warburton, and later used by the American Sail Training Association.

Breeze

Designed and built by Ralph Sewell in New Zealand in 1981 and undertakes private sail training cruises from Auckland. She is now based at Coromandel.

Eye of the Wind (steel) (*50*, 57–61, 65)

Built as the *Friedrich*, a 90ft, 137 gross ton topsail schooner by C Lühring at Hammelwarden, a small village on the River Weser near Brake, W Germany in 1911. She was built for deep-sea work, taking salt from Europe to the River Plate and returning with South American hides, but probably only made a few Plate voyages. Originally she was based in Hamburg, then Rostock after World War I. She was sold to Swedish owners in 1925 and shortly afterwards had her first engine fitted, under the name *Sam* and then *Merry*. She went herring fishing off Iceland from the Swedish west coast port of Gronsund; she went aground in the 1950s and had some of her bottom plates renewed. In 1956 she became the *Rose-Marie* but reverted later to *Merry*. In 1970 there was a bad fire aboard and she was laid up at Gothenburg, Sweden. Bought in 1973 by a group led by Tony 'Tiger' Timbs of London, she was taken to Grimsby and then Faversham where she was registered and completely rigged out as a brigantine. In October 1976 sailed on her first charter voyage and made 2½ circumnavigation voyages round the world. One of these voyages was the Operation Drake voyage in which 216 young people took part in different legs of the expedition over two years. In 1984 she was based at Sydney, Australia.

Golden Plover (iron) (62)
Built as a steamer in 1910 at Melbourne, Australia. She was damaged by fire and bought in 1970 by G & H Jacovry and rebuilt as a brigantine. She sailed round the world and returned to do charter work at Whitsunday Passage. She is now owned by John de Vere, and is based at Airlie Beach, Queensland.

Ji Fung
A 110ft brigantine built by Kong & Haivorsen at Hong Kong in 1980. Her name means 'Spirit of Resolution'. She is operated by the Hong Kong Outward Bound School.

Lillibjorn
Built as a motor trading ketch in Gilillie, Denmark, in 1953. She was later sold to British owners and rigged as the schooner *Christian Bach* in Leith, then she was sold to an Australian owner who converted her to a brigantine at Inverness. Later she was sold back to Denmark and then sailed to the West Indies for cruise work.

Pathfinder (steel) (62)
Built on the same lines at *St Lawrence II* by Toronto Brigantine Incorporated in 1963 for young people to sail on in the Canadian Great Lakes. She is based at Toronto.

Phoenix (39)
A jagt-built galease built in Frederikshavn, Denmark in 1929 as the *Gabriel*. She was sold to Dutch owners and converted in 1975 to a brigantine under the Irish flag and based at Massluis, near Rotterdam. In 1982 she was taken over by an English sailmaker and moved to Littlehampton; the following year she sailed for Jamaica for the cruise trade.

Playfair (steel) (62)
Built at Toronto, Ontario, in 1974 by Toronto Brigantine Incorporated on the lines of *St Lawrence II*, but fitted with central heating and better accommodation for sailing in the Upper Lakes. She is based at Toronto.

Romance (52, 53, 62–5)
A jagt-built galease built by Ring Andersen in 1936 as the *Grethe*. In 1964 she was converted to an 1840-style brigantine *Thetis* for the film 'Hawaii', she was sailed from Holbaek to Hawaii by Captain Alan Villiers. In 1966 she was sold to an American, Captain Arthur M Kimberly, and based at St Thomas, Virgin Islands, for West Indian cruises. Captain Kimberly also ran a scheme training young people in square rig sailing. The

The brigantine *Søren Larsen* pays her way with film work and adventure cruises. *Author*

Romance sometimes leaves her normal charter routes for longer voyages and has twice sailed round the world. In 1984, she was still based at St Thornes.

Søren Larsen (126, *139*)
Built as a motor ketch at Nykøbing Mors, Denmark in 1949 for the Lim Fjord-Copenhagen trade. Cruiser sterned, she is 105ft long and 149 gross tons. She was sold to British owners in 1970s and damaged by fire at Faversham. Later she was bought by Robin and Anthony Davies and rigged out as a brigantine at Colchester, Essex in 1979. She is based at Brightlingsea for charter work, mostly to film companies, and was on charter to the Jubilee Sailing Trust from 1983.

St Lawrence II (steel) (46, 62)
A 59ft vessel built to the design by Francis MacLachlan at Kingston, Ontario, in 1953, and named after a 112-gun man-of-war built for the Royal Navy at Kingston in 1814. The *St Lawrence II* is sailed on the Great Lakes by the Royal Canadian Sea Cadet Corps, and is based at Kingston.

Taiyo (steel)
A brigantine setting only two square sails on the foremast. She was built in 1978 and operated by Ocean Voyages of Sausalito, California for cruising and diving in the Pacific.

Wilhelm Pieck (steel)
Built in 1950 as a training ship for the East German government and named after the first president of the German Democratic Republic. She has a displacement of around 290 tons and has a total crew of forty-five. She is based at Greifswald.

Young America (ferro-cement)
Built at Port Jefferson, New York, in 1976 as the *Enchantress*, and later a sail training brigantine based at Atlantic City.

Zelu
A 73ft jagt-built galease built by A B Holms at Raa in 1938. After trading finished she was taken to Portsmouth and was partly converted to a yacht. She was bought in 1983 by Nick Broughton and taken to be near the International Boat Building Centre at Lake Lothing, Lowestoft. She has been rigged out as a brigantine for a four-year round-the-world charter voyage for Operation Raleigh, a follow on from Operation Drake.

Schooners

Active
Built by Ring Andersen, Svendborg in 1951 as the motor schooner *Mona*. She was rigged out as a three-masted topsail schooner at Troense, Denmark, in 1980 for charter work. Her owner is Volkwin Marg of Hamburg who also owns the galease *Marie* and the skûtje *Fortuna*.

Adventure (110)
A Grand Bank fishing schooner built at Essex, Massachusetts in 1926, measuring 118ft long, and 134 gross tons. She made her last fishing voyage using dories in 1954 and was the last American schooner from Gloucester to do this. She was then rebuilt for the cruise trade from Camden and is now owned by Jim Sharp.

Albatros
A 94ft wooden clipper-built trading schooner built with an engine at Hobro, Denmark in 1942. Named *Esther Lohse* after the first owner's wife, she spent her first eleven years in the Greenland and Iceland trades. Later she spent four years as a 'stone fisher' dredging up stone for the construction of a breakwater for the Kiel Olympics. In 1973 she was bought by Robin Davies and taken to Brightlingsea where she was redecked and converted to a three-masted topsail schooner by Anthony Davies. In 1978 she was sold to Deutscher Schulschiff-Verein (German STA), sailed to Bremerhaven and renamed *Albatros*.

Albatross (steel)
A steel vessel built at Gothenburg in 1942 as a cargo-carrying sail training vessel; in effect she was a motor ship with four masts. She only undertook a few short trips in World War II, but in the 1950–60s

she was making long ocean voyages. All sails and bowsprit were removed in 1967 when she became the *Donna* and, later, the *Dorothea*. Bought by the British Department of Trade in the late 1970s she became the Fishery Support Vessel *Miranda*. She was sold to German owners in 1981 and left Hull for Lübeck for conversion to a cruise schooner in the West Indies.

Alma Doepel
Built as a three-masted topsail schooner on Bellinger River, New South Wales, for the Australia-New Zealand trade. Her square sails were removed in 1937 and an auxiliary engine fitted. During World War II, she was converted to a motor ship and used as a US army supply vessel in the Pacific. She was rigged out again after the war and was in the Tasmanian trade until bought by Sail & Adventure of Melbourne for conversion to a training ship. Her home port is Melbourne.

America
Built at East Boothbay, Maine in 1967 as a 104ft replica of the famous schooner *America* which won the America Cup in 1851. The replica was originally a yacht but in 1982 was on charter at Antigua under the Spanish flag. Her home port is Nelson's Harbour, Antigua.

Anny (steel)
Built by C Lühring near Brake, Germany in 1914. Her maiden voyage was to Russia where she was caught by World War I and remained until 1925 when she was bought by another German owner and renamed *Hanna*. She was bought by Captain Max Both in 1936 and renamed *Kuth Both*. In 1950 she was lengthened from 94ft to 130ft and converted to a motorship. In 1957 acquired by Swedish owners and became the *Ringo* and in 1963 came under the Finnish flag. She was bought in 1980 by the Germania Schiffahrt Gmbh of Hamburg and converted to a three-masted schooner with a yard for a square sail on the foremast, in preparation for the West Indies cruise trade.

Appledore
Built by Harvey Gamage, Bristol, Maine in 1978 for cruise work. As a new schooner she took two years to circumnavigate the world; she is now in the Maine cruise trade.

Aquila Marina
Three-masted topsail schooner built at Nyborg, Denmark in 1920 with a jagt hull. In about 1968 bought by Peter Baker as *Als* and taken to St Germans, Cornwall, England. Sold in 1974 for conversion to a restaurant and then to the Grand Prix racing driver Jochen Maas. He had her refitted and rigged out in Spain and Sète, southern France, as a base ship for diving in the Mediterranean, although the schooner has been registered in Guernsey.

Atlantis Adventure
Built in Norway in 1911 as a fishing boat, probably a motor sailer. Came to England as the *Kobben* and was converted to a schooner at Dartmouth, for the Atlantis Commune of Inishfree, Co Donegal.

Bel Espoir II
Built by J Ring Andersen, Svendborg, in 1944 as the Danish three-masted trading schooner *Nellie S*. Later she traded as the *Peder Most* until 1955 when she became the British training schooner *Prince Louis*. She operated for the Outward Bound School from Burghead, Elgin and later for the Dulverton Trust from the Clyde. In 1968 she was sold to Amis de Jeudi-Dimanche

The French Navy's topsail schooner *Belle Poule* off Cap Frehel, Brittany during the Parade of Sail, 1984. *Author*

and based in Brittany under her present name as a training ship.

Belle Poule (30, *45*, *141*)
Built at Fecamp in 1932, rebuilt in 1975 as a training ship of the French Navy, based on the lines of a Paimpol schooner in the Icelandic fishery. Her hull however is more fine lined than the fishing schooners. She has the traditional French single square topsail which is furled from the deck by roller reefing, worked by chains. Her home port is Brest.

Berta of Ibiza
Trading schooner built at Ibiza, Balearic Island, Spain in 1945, 110ft long 162 gross tons. In late 1970s she was bought by American owners, registered in Panama and rebuilt. In 1979 she crossed the Atlantic with a cargo of antique furniture; on arrival she loaded cargo in Brooklyn for Trinidad, thus becoming the first sailing ship to load in New York since the four-masted schooner *Constellation* sailed for South Africa in 1943 and was wrecked on a reef off Bermuda on passage. *Berta* was registered as a merchant ship under the Panamanian flag owned by (US) Shilon Navigation Co.

Bill of Rights (110, 112)
Cruise schooner built on the lines of a Baltimore clipper in 1971. This 125ft schooner carries 34 passengers in the cruise trade.

Bowdoin (110)
An exploration schooner similar to a Gloucester knockabout schooner, built at East Boothbay, Maine, in 1921. This 87ft, 66 gross ton vessel sailed into the Arctic every summer until World War II. She was used for patrolling in Greenland with the US Navy in World War II and then returned to Arctic expeditions under Admiral MacMillion. She was handed over to Mystic Seaport, Connecticut and later used for the cruise trade.

Brabander (steel)
Built in England in 1978 for the Dutch De Brabantse Zeil School of Drimmelen Yacht Haven, The Netherlands. She is a 92ft topsail schooner built on yacht lines and has painted gun ports.

Britta Leth
Jagt-built Baltic trader built at Oxenbjerg in 1911. In 1983 this Danish schooner set square sails flying on the foremast.

Californian
A 92ft schooner built at Spanish landing, San Diego, California and launched in 1984. She was designed by Melbourne Smith on the lines of the topsail schooner *Lawrence*, the first Revenue cutter on the west coast. Her home port is San Diego.

Carene
Baltic trader built by Ring Andersen, Svendborg as the *Lars* in 1945. In 1978 she was converted to a three-masted topsail schooner for French owners.

Creole (composite) (46)
A three-masted staysail schooner yacht built in 1927 by Camper & Nicholson, Cowes. The teak on steel hull is 189ft long and 433 gross tons. She belonged to British owners before World War II, but in 1951 was bought by the Greek ship owner Stavros Niarchos. In about 1978, she was acquired by the Twin School, Nyborg as a part of their sail training fleet. In 1983 she was sold to Italian owners and sailed for Sicily.

Creoula II (steel) (*142*)
Built in 1937 at Lisbon as a four-masted Portuguese Grand Bank schooner, and still sailing to the Grand Banks in 1972 when she had a crew of 68 men of which 54 were fishermen. She was then owned

The Portuguese Grand Bank schooner *Creoula* lying off her owners' cod drying plant at Barreiro near Lisbon in 1972. She is loaded with salt and is about to cross the Atlantic – virtually the last time a sail using vessel made this century-old voyage. *Author*

by Parceria Geral de Pescarias, Lisbon, but later she was converted to a training ship.

Dayspring

Built for the Maine charter trade at North End Shipyard in 1984 by her owners Bill and Judy Wasson. Her home port is Camden, but she winters in St Thomas, Virgin Islands.

De Wadden (steel)

116ft three-masted Dutch trading schooner built at Waterhuizen, the Netherlands in 1917, and later bought by Hall of Arklow, the Irish port which became a stronghold of motor sailing vessels from 1920–1950s. In World War II she made several voyages to Portugal, but was chiefly in the coal trade from Garston on the River Mersey. This trade finished in the late 1960s and the De Wadden was sold to an owner on the Clyde. She was used to load sand ballast in the Kyles of Bute which was sold at her home port of Dunoon. When the authorities ordered this to stop in 1977 she was the last British-owned schooner in commercial work. She was later used for angling trips in the Clyde, and still had her original panelled after cabins. Her home port is Dunoon.

Elinor

A Danish jagt-built (sloping transom stern and round bow) trading schooner built in 1906 at Stubbekøbing, 83ft 72 tons. She was rigged out as a three-masted topsail schooner and in 1980 made an Atlantic voyage with fare-paying crew.

Elise (steel)

A Dutch fishing logger built by Vigee at Massluis in 1917. She was later lengthened to about 110ft and fished from Scheveningen as the *Meester Johan Last*. In 1980 Johan Hazehamp started work on converting her to a four-masted schooner at Enkhuizen for charter work. She is currently based at Enkhuizen.

Ernestina

A 97ft fishing schooner built at Essex, Massachusetts, as the *Effie M Morrissey*. She fished until 1926 and was then sold to Captain William Bartlet who commanded her in 21 polar explorations.

She was later sold to the Portuguese who put her back into fishing and later still she became the *Ernestina*, carrying passengers – mostly immigrants – and freight from the Cape Verde Islands off the West Coast of Africa to Providence, Rhode Island. She was laid up after the packet trade finished and in 1976 funds were raised in the United States and by the Cape Verde Government to enable her to return to the States for preservation. The schooner sailed for the States but was dismasted in a gale and had to put back. A more thorough restoration was then made, supervised by the Dutch shipwright Frans Meijer who made a seventeen-day passage from Lisbon to Cape Verde with hardware on his rebuilt Portuguese fishing schooner *Sejas Feliz*. In 1982 *Ernestina* was sailed back to New Bedford, Massachusetts for further restoration.

Esmeralda (steel) (37, 42)

Built at Cadiz, Spain in 1952 as a training ship for the Chilean Navy. This 308ft four-masted vessel has been the subject of a great deal of argument as to whether the four square sails on the foremast make her a schooner or a barquentine; she has, however, the long foremast of a schooner. Her home port is Valparaiso.

Falken (steel)

Built in 1946 at the Naval Dockyard, Stockholm as a two-masted training schooner for the Royal Swedish Navy. She sometimes sets a square sail on the foremast, and is used for training both Royal and Merchant Navy cadets. Her home port is Karlskrona.

Fantome (steel) (90, 91, 92)

Built as a four-masted gaff schooner on the lines of an American multi-masted cargo schooner at Livorno, Italy, in 1929 as the yacht *Flying Cloud* for the Duke of Westminster. From 1937–56 she was the yacht *Fantome III* and was then laid up. She was bought by Mike Burke's Windjammer Cruises and converted at Miami, Florida to a four-masted staysail schooner for the West Indies cruise trade. She started work in about 1971 with a crew of 30 and 130 passengers.

Flying Cloud (steel) (91)
Built at Nantes by Dubigeon in 1935 as the 420-ton three-masted gaff schooner *Oiseau des Îles*. She was used by the French as an expedition and cadet ship in the South Pacific. Next she became a motor coaster under the Mexican flag until sold to Mike Burke's Windjammer Cruises in 1965. She has been converted to the staysail schooner *Flying Cloud* but has some square sails on the foremast. She cruises in the West Indies with a crew of 20 and 80 passengers.

Freia (steel)
A clipper-built Danish trading schooner built in 1897. She was based on the Island of Bornholm, and converted back to a schooner in the late 1970s at Rudkøbing. In 1983 she was based on Turö for charter work under the Panamanian flag, but Danish-owned.

Frya (steel)
A clipper-built three-masted topsail schooner built at Marstal, Denmark, in 1907 as the *Olaf Petersen*. In 1984 she was based at Amsterdam for charter work.

Fulton
Built in 1915 at Marstal, Denmark as a jagt-built trading schooner. She was originally Danish-owned, but was later sold to Swedish owners and fitted with a two cylinder oil engine. About 1958 she was sold to owners in Aalborg, Denmark.

In 1970 she was bought by the Danish National Maritime Museum and rigged out again as a three-masted schooner.

Fylla
The last wooden Greenland trader to be built at Nyborg, Denmark (1930). In 1983 she became a three-masted schooner with one yard on the foremast and was based at Svendborg as a youth training ship for the Island of Fyn.

Gefion (*39*, 59)
A jagt-built Danish trading schooner built in 1894. She was later rebuilt by owners from Lübeck, Germany and rigged out as a topsail schooner. She took part in the 1976 Transatlantic Tall Ships Race, and was later sold to a Belgian diving club.

Gladen (steel)
Built at Stockholm in 1947 as a sister ship to the *Falken* as a training schooner for the Royal Swedish Navy. She was overall winner of the 1972 Helsinki-Falsterbo Tall Ships Race. Her home port is Karlskrona.

Godewind (steel)
A three-masted schooner launched by C Luhring on the river Weser, Germany in 1915. Apparently she lay uncompleted for two years and sailed as the *Landkirchen*. In 1921 she was lengthened to 110ft. By 1955 she was trading as a motor ship. This finished in 1975 and in 1983 she was converted to the *Godewind* for the cruise trade in the Windward Islands in the West Indies under German ownership.

Grossherzogin Elizabeth (steel)
Dutch three-masted trading schooner built as the *San Antonia* by Jan Smit, Albasserdam, The Netherlands with a diesel auxiliary in 1909. She became the Rotterdam motorship *Ariadne* and in the 1970s was converted back to a three-masted schooner for German owners and made voyages to the West Indies. In 1982 she was sold to the German Merchant Marine Academy and given the name of one of their previous training ships, a full rigged ship built in 1901. Her home port is Elsfleth.

Harvey Gamage (110, 112, *144*)
A 95ft schooner built in 1973 by Harvey Gamage, South Bristol, for Eben

The Maine cruise schooner *Harvey Gamage* was named after her well known South Bristol builder. *A O Dannenberg*

Whitcomb for work in the cruise trade from Clinton Harbor, Connecticut in the summer and in the winter in the Virgin Islands. In 1984, she was still based at Clinton Harbour.

Helga
A jagt-built Baltic trader brought to Faversham, Kent in the 1970s. She was damaged by fire and then bought by Alan Reekie who rebuilt her at the Iron Bridge Wharf, Faversham. She started sailing in 1983 as a two-masted schooner. She is based at Faversham.

Isaac H Evans (111)
A 64ft schooner built in 1886 as a Delaware Bay oyster schooner. She was rebuilt at Percy & Small Shipyard and owned by Bath Marine Museum. She is now part of the Maine cruise trade.

Janet May
A 65ft Maine charter schooner built on the lines of a coasting schooner on the Narraguagas River in 1984.

Jaques Cartier (composite)
Built in 1942 in Germany as a motor-sail patrol vessel and later became a trawler. She was converted to the topsail schooner Le Marsouin by John Cluett of Guernsey in 1982, and given the name Jaques Cartier when on charter to the St Malo Mariners Association.

J & E Riggin (109)
An 89ft oyster schooner built in Dorchester, New Jersey in 1927. In 1976 she was rebuilt at Doug Lea's North End Yard, Rockland, for the Maine cruise trade. Her home port is Rockland, Maine.

Johanna Lucretia (63)
Built as a Belgian trawler in 1945. She was later bought by a Dutchman, Ber van Meer, and converted to a schooner. In about 1977 she started taking long voyages with charter parties from Enkuizen; she is often seen in British waters.

Juan Sebastian De Elcano (steel) (42)
A four-masted topsail schooner built at Cadiz, Spain, as a training ship for the Spanish Navy in 1927.

Julia
A Danish three-masted trading schooner built at Faaborg in 1938. She later became the three-masted Jetta Jan. She was

considered to be beyond repair, however, Jacobsen Plads, Troense Yard, rebuilt her as the topsail schooner Julia of Faaborg for the Baltic charter trade. In 1983 she was German-owned, but flying the British flag and registered in Gibraltar.

Lady Ellen (steel)
A topgallant schooner built at Vindo, Sweden in 1981 and owned by Lars Johansson. She is a replica of Ellen, a schooner built in 1909 and owned by Mr Johansson's father.

L'Etoile (30)
Built as a Naval training ship at Fecamp, North France in 1932, as a topsail schooner. She is a sister ship to the Belle Poule, and was rebuilt in 1975. Her home port is Brest.

Lewis R French (111)
Former cargo schooner, built in 1871 and rebuilt in 1976 at Rockland, Maine for the cruise trade. In 1984 she was sailing from Rockland Harbor taking groups of 22 guests. She sets 3000sq ft of sail including two topsails.

Lilla Dan
Built in 1950 by Ring Andersen, Svendborg as a jagt-built topsail schooner for the sail training scheme based at Svendborg. In 1983 she was undertaking some summer charter work.

Lindo (39)
Built as a jagt-built trader in 1929. She was rerigged as a smart three-masted topsail schooner owned by Canadians and registered in the Grand Cayman Islands in the mid-1970s. She took part in the 1976 and 1980 Tall Ships Races across the North Atlantic, and later did charter work in the West Indies. In 1983 she was bought by the City of Alexandria on the Potomac River, Virginia, USA.

Malcolm Miller (steel) (46, 58)
Built at Aberdeen in 1968 as a 134ft, three-masted topsail schooner for the Sail Training Association. She sails most of the year on fortnightly cruises between different ports in the British Isles with a crew of young people. The Malcolm Miller has entered many Tall Ships Races. Her home port is Portsmouth.

Marie Galante (steel)
Built as a German herring drifting logger in 1907. In 1983 she was a Dutch cruise schooner, based at Enkhuizen.

Mary Day (110)
An 83ft schooner built in 1962 by Harvey Gamage, on the lines of a cargo schooner like *Stephen Taber* and *Mattie*. She sails in the Maine cruise trade carrying 28 passengers.

Mattie (110)
Built as the freighter *Grace Bailey* at Patchogue, New York in 1882. 81ft long and 58 tons. She has been in the cruise trade since the 1930s and operates from Camden, Maine.

Mercandic II
Baltic trader built as the *Talata* by Ring Andersen, Svendborg in 1942. 97ft long and 100 tons. She was bought by Per Henridsen of Mercandia Shipping Ltd, Copenhagen and converted in 1975–77 at Svendborg to a three-masted topsail schooner for publicity voyages.

Mercantile (110)
Built as a freight carrier at Deer Isle, Maine in 1916. 78ft long, 41 gross tons. She carries 28 passengers in the Maine cruise trade out of Camden.

Meta
A 46ft clipper-built Danish trading schooner built by H Christophersen at Assens in 1884. She traded in the Baltic and then became a stone fisher. In 1983 she was being rebuilt at Rudkøbing by Ole Mortenson and his partner. She is currently based at Rudkøbing.

Midsommer (steel) (105)
Built in 1910 at Vlaardingen, The Netherlands, as the Dutch fishing logger *Johanna Jacoba*. She became a Baltic cargo vessel and in the 1970s was converted to a charter schooner at Troense, Denmark. The logger was a gaff ketch with a loose-footed mainsail used for herring drifting. Her home port is Flensburg.

Mistress
Built in 1977 by Reginald Eaton of Stonington, Maine. She is a 40ft schooner which carries six passengers in the Maine cruise trade.

New Endeavour (56–57, 58, 61, 62)
Built as the *Dana* by Ring Andersen, Svendborg in 1919. She was bought as the *Cito* by a British-Australian group and taken to Ramsgate, England in 1965. Later sailed out to Australia as a three-masted topsail schooner. Based at Sydney and used for film work. She was laid up, unseaworthy, for a long period but in 1983 was sailing again, and was still based at Sydney.

Orionia
Built in 1896 as the Spanish trading schooner *Joven Therese* and rebuilt in 1964. After being rerigged as a schooner, she started sailing in 1983.

Outlaw
Built in the Balearic Islands, Spain in 1959 as the *Antonio Matutis*. In the late 1970s she was sold to German owners and registered in Malta. In 1983 she was in the Mediterranean making training voyages for young people with social problems.

Pascual Flores
106ft beamy Spanish trading schooner built as a three-masted topsail schooner at Torrevieja on the Mediterranean coast in 1918. She was intended for the fruit trade between the Balearic Islands and the mainland. She had a reputation for speed and won local schooner races; she was later in the salt trade. She was laid up in the Spanish Civil War and was rebuilt

The British *Golden Cachalot* in the Galapagos Islands. Because of the damage caused to wild life in the Galapagos most foreign-owned ships were stopped from operating charter cruises so after five years the *Golden Cachalot* switched to Belize in British Honduras. *Roger Jameson*

and converted to a motorship in 1946. In 1975 she was bought by Peter Gregson and taken to Dartmouth. There she had her masts stepped as a two-masted schooner. She was later bought by the Nova Charitable Trust for youth sail training from Bristol, England. In 1983 she was in dry dock at the Albion Shipyard, Bristol, undergoing a slow refit.

Pioneer (steel)
Built on the River Delaware as a gaff trading sloop in 1885. She was rerigged as a schooner and rebuilt in 1968 and is operated from the South Street Seaport Museum, in New York by the Pioneer Marine Schooner organization.

Pirata
Built at Mallorca, Spain in 1938. In the 1970s John Cluett of Guernsey converted her to the topsail schooner *El Pirata* for charter work. She took part in the 1980 Boston-Kristiansand Tall Ships Race and sold in 1982 to Swiss owners.

Polynesia (steel) (91)
Built by De Haan & Oerlmans, Heusden, the Netherlands in 1938 as the four-masted, 413-tons net Portuguese Grand Banker *Argus*. She carried 72 crew and 53 dories. Every spring she sailed from Lisbon to fish on the Grand Banks and in the Greenland Strait through the summer and returned in the autumn loaded with salted cod. By 1970 she was laid up and in 1973 was bought by Mike Burke's Windjammer Cruises and converted into a staysail schooner renamed *Polynesia* for holiday cruise work in the West Indies. She has a crew of 30 and holds up to 126 passengers.

Pride of Baltimore (112)
Built on the lines of a Baltimore clipper by Melbourne Smith to a design by Thomas C Gillmer at an improvised yard in Baltimore's Inner Harbor in 1977. She is owned by the City of Baltimore and with a crew of 12 makes goodwill cruises around North America.

Prince Louis
Built at Svendborg in 1921 as a trading schooner. She ended her trading life as the motorship *Lille Baelt*. She was bought in

1969 by two Americans, rerigged as a three-masted schooner and sailed out to Los Angeles.

Rachael and Ebenezer (ferro-cement) (110, 111)
A 105ft charter schooner built at Bath, Maine in 1973.

Richard Robbins Sr (77)
A 56ft Delaware Bay oyster dredging schooner built at Greenwich, New Jersey in 1902. In 1966 she was sold to become a Maine cruise ship and in 1976 was being rebuilt at North End Yard, Rockland, Maine.

Roseway (110)
112ft Boston pilot schooner built in 1925. She is now a cruise schooner working in the fleet from Camden, Maine.

Semper Volaers (steel)
A schooner built by Bodewes at Martenshoek, The Netherlands, in 1910 as the *Amalie*. She traded first under German and then Danish flags. Around 1979 she was converted back to a three-masted schooner at Enkhuizen and began cruise work. In 1983 she was sold to Tahiti owners and sailed for the Pacific.

The Lunenburg fishing schooner *Uda R Corkum* racing. She was a spoon bowed 'saltbanker' which went dory fishing in the summer and was lost with twenty men on Sable Island in August 1927. *Nova Scotia Museum*

The Finnish-built schooner *Stina* now operates from Ipswich where dock and railway link make a convenient home port for charter work. *Author*

Shabab Oman

A three-masted topgallant schooner built by Herd & MacKenzie, Buckie, Scotland in 1971 as the *Captain Scott*. 104ft long, 380 tons displacement, designed by Robert Clarke, her frames are of oak and planking of larch. She was based at Plockton, Ross-shire, making 26-day cruises on the West Coast of Scotland during the 1970s which included mountaineering expeditions. In 1978 she was sold to the Sultan of Oman to continue as a training ship under the name *Youth of Oman*.

Shenandoah (110, 112)

A topsail schooner, built on the lines of a US Revenue cutter *Joe Lane* built in 1848, at Harvey Gamage's in 1964. She was originally in the cruise trade from Vineyard Haven, Massachusetts.

Sir Winston Churchill (steel) (46, 58)

Built at Hessle on the River Humber, England, in 1966 as a three-masted topsail schooner for the Sail Training Association. She spends most of the year on two week cruises with young people between different British and near Continental ports. Her home port is Portsmouth. Both the STA schooners regularly take part in the Tall Ships Races.

Stephen Taber (110, 111)

A 68ft schooner built in 1871 at Glenwood Landing, New York for hauling bricks and general freight on the Hudson River. In 1936 she was taken to Maine by

Captain Fred Wood and used to haul pulpwood to the mills in Bucksport. She was later sold to Captain Guild and converted for the cruise trade, based at Camden. She was bought by Captain Ken Barnes in 1979 and in 1982 hauled out at North End Shipyard, Rockland, for a major refit.

Stina of Sipoo (148)

A 75ft Finnish trader built in 1946. She was fitted with an engine in 1952 and worked mostly in the sand trade, but was involved in smuggling at one stage. In 1976 she was brought to Ipswich, England and later bought by Mike Little and Hilary Levy and rigged as a schooner at Maldon. In 1982 she was based at Ipswich for charter work. She went to Lisbon in 1982 for the 25th Anniversary of the Tall Ships Races; she also took part in the 1983 Travemunde-Karlskrona Tall Ships Race.

Svanen

Built by Ring Andersen in 1916. She traded under the Norwegian and Swedish flags in fish and timber until 1964, when a group from Kristiansand in Southern Norway purchased her for preservation. In 1972 she was sold to the Norwegian Maritime Museum and is now based at Oslo.

Sylvina W Beal

Built in 1911 in East Boothbay and converted to a power sardine netter in the 1930s. In 1981 this schooner was rebuilt and had an engine installed at Belfast, Maine for the cruise trade.

Thor Heyerdahl (steel)

Built as a Dutch motor coaster by E Smit & Zoon at Westerbroek in 1931. Lengthened in 1951 to 127ft. She seems to have had several names – *Tinka*, *Marga Henning*, *Silke* and *Minnow*. She was converted to a three-masted topsail schooner and given the name *Thor Heyerdahl* because the German owner had sailed with the Norwegian adventurer of this name. She can carry 28 passengers. She spent the summer of 1983 working in the Baltic from Kiel and in the autumn sailed for the West Indies.

Timberwind (110)

Built in 1931 as a 69ft pilot schooner for

Portland, Maine. She was later fitted out for cruises from Camden, Maine.

Undine (steel) (107)

A Dutch motor coaster setting one mast and sail, built as the *Francisca* at Delfzijl in 1931. She was later lengthened to take a load of 120 tons. She was bought by Joachim Kaiser and taken to the shipyard at Gluckstadt on the River Elbe and the lengthened section was removed. This shipyard had previously lengthened many coasters. In 1984 after four years work the *Undine* was to be rigged as a typical Dutch trading schooner. She is to carry young people with social problems and in order to give the voyages a purpose, 80 tons of cargo will be loaded. Her home port is Gluckstadt.

Vale de Moura

Built as a salt carrier S101 TL at Setubal, Portugal in 1956. She sailed to Bremerhaven, Germany in 1981, where she was totally rebuilt and rigged in 1983. She is currently still based at Bremerhaven.

Victory Chimes (111, 112)

Three-masted centreboard schooner built in 1900 at Bethel, Delaware, as the Chesapeake Bay 'ram' *Edwin & Maud*. 132ft and 208 gross tons. She was bought in 1954 by Captain Frederick Guild of Castine, Maine, to replace his previous *Victory Chimes*. She is the only three-master in the Maine cruise trade and is based at Camden.

Vidar

Three-masted trading schooner built at Bergen, Norway in 1877. She is now German-owned and based at Busum.

Voyager

65ft New England cruise schooner built in 1978. She carries twenty passengers.

Wander Bird

German pilot schooner built by Stulcken, Hamburg, in 1881 as the *Elbe 5* – one of seven schooners built before 1900 for pilots who waited out in the North Sea for ships working into the River Elbe. She was laid up in 1924, bought in 1927 by Warwick Tompkins and sailed round Cape Horn from Gloucester, Massachusetts to San Francisco in 121 days. She later became a houseboat. She was bought in 1969 by tug skipper Harold Sommer, and restored and sailed again in 1981. Her home port is San Francisco.

Yankee Clipper (steel) (90, 91)

Built in 1927 at Krupp's Germanic Werft, Kiel, Germany as the 180-ton net yacht *Cressida* for Fredrick Krupp. She was taken by the USA as a war prize in 1945. She became the two-masted staysail schooner *Yankee Clipper* for Windjammer Cruises in the West Indies.

The *Enterprize* was one of the early cruise schooners in Maine, USA.

Chesapeake Bay Skipjacks licenced to dredge oysters and believed active in the 1983 season

Name	Place of Building	Date
Anna McGarvey (81)	Annapolis, Md	1980
Caleb W Jones (80)	Reedville, Va	1953
City of Crisfield (80)	Reedville, Va	1949
Clarence Crockett	Deep Creek, Va	1908

Dee of St Marys (81)	Piney Point, Md	1979
E C Collier (75, 76–78)	Deal Island, Md	1910
Elsworth	Hudson, Md	1901
Fanny J Daughtery	Crisfield, Md	1904
F C Lewis	Hopkins, Va	1907
Hilda M Willing	Oriole, Md	1905
H M Krentz (78, 80)	Harryhogan, Va	1955
Howard	Deep Creek, Va	1909
Ida Mae	Urbanna, Va	1898
Kathryn	Crisfield, Md	1901
Lady Joanne (Formerly *Lady Agnes*)	Oxford, Md	1968
Lady Katie (75, 76–78, 80)	Wingate, Md	1956
Lorraine Rose (80)	Reedville, Va	1949
Martha Lewis (76, 80)	Wingate, Md	1955
Minnie V (81)	Wenona, Md	1906
Nellie L Byrd	Oriole, Md	1911
Ralph T Webster	Oriole, Md	1905
Rebecca T Ruark (78)	Taylors Island, Md	1886
Seagull	Crisfield, Md	1924
Somerset (80)	Reedville, Va	1949
Stanley Norman (80)	Salisbury, Md	1902
Susan Mae (78)	Pocomoke City, Md	1901
Thomas Clyde	Oriole, Md	1911
Wilma Lee	Wingate, Md	1940

In 1984 the *Connie Francis* was being built by Francis Goddard at Piney Point, Maryland. The *Rosie Parks* was at the Chesapeake Bay Maritime Museum, St Michaels, Maryland; this museum spent five years rebuilding the bugeye *Edna E Lockwood*, built in 1889. The bugeye was a round bottomed ketch with sharp-headed sails, not gaff like the round-bottomed Chesapeake Bay sloops. The *Sallie Bramble*, a bugeye with a skipjack rig, had been sold for exhibition at Port Tobacco Alternative for Learning Centre which already owns the *Claud W Somers*.

The *Norfolk*, a 71ft skipjack built at Deal Island in 1900, which dredged under sail under the name *George W Collier* is used for Sail Training, supported by the City of Norfolk, Nautical Adventures Inc, private businesses and other citizens.

British Coastal Traders

At the turn of this century the small coastal ports of Britain were packed with trading schooners, ketches and smacks. The following vessels have survived until recent years.

Emily Barratt (*96*)
Built at Millom, Cumbria in 1913. This was then a thriving mining port which has now silted up. She has the pointed stern typical of the Irish Sea schooners and was the last round-bottomed trader built in Britain. Soon converted to a ketch, then fitted with an auxiliary, she became one of the motor ketches owned in the Appledore area of north Devon, trading in the Bristol Channel. She was sold to become a yacht and moved to St Osyth's, Essex in about 1962; later she became a houseboat at Mistley, Brightlingsea and St Katharine's Dock, London until George Patterson bought her in 1983. She then moved to Cook's Yard, Maldon, Essex for a major refit to be used for sail training from Maryport, Cumbria. *Brains ?*

Fjordbo (steel)
Built as a three-masted motor schooner at Amlwch, a tiny mining port on the Isle of Anglesey, as the *Eilian* in 1908. She was

originally in the Welsh slate trade to British and near Continental ports. In 1928 she was sold to owners in Braunton, north Devon. After World War II she was mostly in the coal trade across the Bristol Channel. Sold to Danish owners in 1957, she was converted to a motor ship. She lost her clipper bow after a collision, and was later sold and taken out to the West Indies. In 1980 she was owned at Bridgetown, Barbados.

Forsoget

Built as the British trading ketch *Bessie Ellen* by Kelly of Plymouth in 1907. She was trading as a motor ketch after World War II and then sold in 1947 to Danish owners; she then traded as *Forsoget*. In the late 1970s she was totally rebuilt at Troense, Denmark, but in 1984 had still not been rigged out.

Garlandstone

Built between 1903–1909 at Calstock on the Devon side of the River Tamar as a trading ketch by James Goss's Shipyard. She was sold new to Captain Russan of Studdulph, Milford Haven, Pembrokeshire. Her first engine was a twin cylinder paraffin, fitted in 1912, but she was kept under full sail. Her 64 shares were gradually sold to Gloucester interests and in 1920 she became the sole property of Captain Andrew Murdock. In 1941 Murdock sailed her (with a larger engine) single-handed from Courtmacsherry in southern Ireland to the Bristol Channel to load coal at Lydney. She was skippered in World War II by Micha Leszczynski and owned in Braunton. She stopped trading in 1958 and had several owners who tried to use her as a yacht. She finished up being abandoned on St Patrick's Causeway, Cardigan Bay and was towed into Barmouth. She was later bought by R A Kyffin and Colin Lansdown and towed to Porthmadog; here in 1974 she was opened at Oakeley Slate Wharf as a Museum. In 1979 she was purchased by the National Museum of Wales with the idea of restoring her as a sea-going museum ship. *Cotehele ?*

Hrvat

Built in 1880 at Runcorn for J Foulkes of Runcorn as the *Snowflake*. She was in the Western Ocean (Atlantic) stock fish trade between Newfoundland and the Latin countries and later in the China Clay trade between Cornwall and Mersey ports. In 1936 she was sold to Yugoslavian owners. She was rebuilt after World War II as the motor coaster *Hrvat* and sold in 1970 to St Martin, near Split.

Irene

An 85ft English trading ketch built by F J Carver & Sons at Bridgewater on the River Parrett in Somerset in 1907. She is a typical coastal ketch of the Edwardian period and was engaged in general trade. One of her better passages was from Teignmouth to Glasgow in five days in 1913. She was owned in Bridgewater for the first ten years then sold to a Swansea owner and fitted with a paraffin auxiliary engine in 1919. In the 1920s work was short on the English coast so she went into the Irish trade. She survived the Irish troubles and the economic slump of the late 1920s and returned to Bridgewater under the ownership of Colthurst Symons for general trade in the Bristol Channel. Her engine size increased and her sails steadily reduced. Under Captain Schiller she remained in trade until 1960 when she was the last British motor ketch to trade. Then she became a yacht owned on the South Coast of England, and was bought in 1971 by Dr Leslie Morrish. Over the years he has steadily rebuilt her including

The *Kathleen & May* as a pole masted motor schooner laid up at Appledore, 1968. Built in 1900 as a three-masted topsail schooner like the *Windermere* by Ferguson & Baird at Connah's Quay, she is now fully restored as part of the Maritime Trust's historic ship collection in St Katharine's Dock, London. *Author*

a major refit at Bristol in 1980–1981. She sailed in the 1982 Tall Ships Race from Falmouth to Lisbon.

Kathleen & May (151)

Built as the *Lizzie May* at Connah's Quay on the River Dee in 1900 as a three-masted topsail schooner and in the general coastal trade. She was sold in 1908 to owners in County Cork and her name was changed to *Kathleen & May*. In 1931 she was bought by Captain Tommy Jewell and his father, William, of Appledore, north Devon. Her square sails were removed and she traded as a motor sailer with pole masts and an 80hp engine. She finished trading in the autumn of 1960 and she was put up for sale at Appledore. She then had various owners including Captain Paul Davies who took her to Barry and tried to get her back into trade. She was bought in 1970 by the Maritime Trust and at Bideford was largely rebuilt

at the expense of Hong Kong shipowner, Y K Pao. In 1971 she was opened to the public at Sutton Pool, Plymouth but did not pay so she was towed to St Katharine's Dock, London to join the Maritime Trust's splendid Historic Ships Collection.

Marie

Built as a trading smack at Salcombe, Devon in 1904. In 1949 she was working as a gravel barge from Appledore. In 1969 she was being used as a houseboat moored in the River Torridge opposite Bideford, and she was still there in 1983.

Result

Built in 1893 at Carrickfergus on Belfast Lough, Northern Ireland as a three-masted topsail schooner. She was in the general coastal trade and became a Q-ship in World War I. She was bought by Clark of Braunton, North Devon in 1928 and slowly cut down to a motor ship with two masts. She was owned by her skipper Captain Peter Welsh, the last of the Westcountry skipper owners, until his death in 1967. In 1970 she was sold to the Ulster Folk Museum for preservation.

Shamrock (87)

Built at Stonehouse, Plymouth by F Hawke in 1899 as a barge to trade in the Rivers Tamar, Plym and Lynher. She seems to have started as a trading smack (gaff cutter) and later became a ketch. In the 1960s she was still trading as a motor barge. In 1972 she was bought by the National Trust and the National Maritime Museum, and rebuilt at Cotehele Quay between 1975–1979. She is kept as a sailing museum ship at the National Trust's Cotehele Quay.

The 'spritty' (spritsail) barge *Marjorie* in the Swin bound from London to Ipswich in 1956 with grain. Without a bowsprit this is a stemhead or staysail rig. *Author*

Spritsail Barges of the East Coast of England

name	place of building	date
Anglia	Ipswich	1898
Ardwina	Ipswich	1909
Beric	Harwich	1896
British Empire	Brightlingsea	1899

British King	Maldon	1901
Cabby (98)	Frindsbury	1928
Cambria	Greenhithe	1906
Centaur (*85*, 88)	Harwich	1895
Convoy (88)	Rye	1900
Dannebrog	Harwich	1901
Dawn (97)	Maldon	1897
Decima	Southampton	1901
Edith May (124, *153*)	Harwich	1906
Ena (98)	Harwich	1906
Ethel	Harwich	1894
Ethel Ada	Ipswich	1897
Ethel Ada	Paglesham	1903
Ethel Maud	Maldon	1889
Felix	Harwich	1893
George Smeed	Rochester	1882
Gladys	Harwich	1901
Hydrogen (98)	Rochester	1906
Ironsides (124, 125)	Grays	1900
Jock	Ipswich	1908
Kimberley	Harwich	1900
Kitty (97, 98)	Harwich	1895
Lady Daphne	Rochester	1923
Lady Gwynfred	Gravesend	1904
Lady of the Lea	Rotherhithe	1931
Lord Roberts (97)	Maldon	1900
Lyford Anna (ex-**Cereal**)	Whitstable	1894
Marjorie (96, 97, *102, 152*)	Ipswich	1902
May (96, 124)	Harwich	1891
Mirosa (124, 125)	Maldon	1892
Montreal	Sittingbourne	1916
Northdown	Whitstable	1924

The *Edith May* leading the Pin Mill Match in 1972 when she was champion of all the barge races for the year. She was sailing with a staysail rig, but that year bowsprits were reintroduced into barge races at the Medway Match. *Author*

The barge *Redoubtable* sailing with new sails after being rigged out at Snape in 1973. In 1982, under the name *David Gestetner*, she got into trouble on a promotion voyage to the Shetlands, was towed in to a Norwegian port and later stripped of her gear. *Author*

Oak	Maldon	1881
Olive May	Sittingbourne	1920
Phoenician	Sittingbourne	1923
Portlight (97)	Mistley	1925
Pudge	Frindsbury	1922
Raybel	Sittingbourne	1920
Remercie	Harwich	1908
Reminder (*121, 125*)	Mistley	1929
Repertor	Mistley	1924
Revival (ex-*Eldred Watkins*)	Ipswich	1901
Scone	Rochester	1919
Scotsman	Sittingbourne	1899
Seagull II	Rochester	1901
Sir Alan Herbert (ex-*Lady Jean*)	Rochester	1926
Spinaway C (*96, 98*)	Ipswich	1899
Thalatta (97)	Harwich	1906
Tollesbury	Sandwich	1901
Venture	Ipswich	1900
Victor	Ipswich	1895
Vigilant (*124*)	Ipswich	1904
Violet	Maldon	1889
Wilfred	East Greenwich	1926
Will (ex-*Will Everard*) (*86*, 98, 126)	Gt Yarmouth	1925
Wyvenhoe	Wivenhoe	1898
Xylonite (*96, 97, 126*)	Mistley	1926

British Working Craft

The following list includes some former British working craft which can be seen sailing in approximately their traditional appearance or have been built to authentic lines.

The Norfolk Wherry Trust's *Albion* at their dyke on Womack Water, Ludham, in 1984. The crew on a wherry live aft in a two berth cuddy. *Author*

name	type	rig	date
Albion (94, *154*)	Norfolk wherry	Wherry rig	1898
Alfred Cory	Lifeboat	Gaff ketch	1893
Alpha	Bristol Channel pilot cutter	Gaff cutter	1904
Amity LN47	Norfolk beach yoll	Gaff cutter	1912
Amy Howson (98)	Humber sloop	Gaff sloop	1914
Annie H1	Scaffie	Dipping lugger	1976
Barnabas SS634	St Ives mackerel driver	Dipping lugger	1881
Baroque	Bristol Channel pilot cutter	Gaff cutter	1902
Black Bess CS32	Solent smack	Gaff cutter	1870
Bonny Tyne	Wear foy boat	Lugger	1977
Caliph LK57	Zulu skiff	Dipping lugger	1905
Carlotta	Bristol Channel pilot cutter	Gaff cutter	1900
Clan Gordon	Loch Fyne skiff		c1910
Comrade (98)	Humber keel	Single mast, square sail	1923
Coronation	Southend beach boat	Gunter sloop	1937
Dolphin	Bristol Channel pilot cutter	Gaff cutter	
Edward & Mary RX74	Hastings beach boat	Dipping lugger	1919
Erin	Mevagissey lugger	Dipping lugger	1904
Fanny CS12	Solent smack	Gaff cutter	1872
Gratitude WY263	Whitby coble	Dipping lugger	1976
Hathor (95)	Norfolk pleasure wherry	Wherry rig	
Hirta	Bristol Channel pilot cutter	Gaff cutter	1911
Isabella Fortuna AH153 (*28, 29*)	Arbroath fifie	Dipping lugger	1890
Irene	Southend beach boat	Sloop	1957
Jeannie	Buckie yoll	Dipping lugger	1929
Joy	Winkle brig	Gaff sloop	1932
Jubilee	Ness sgoth	Dipping lugger	1935
Lady Edith (95)	Norfolk wherry yacht	Wherry rig	1912
Light A395	Rosehearty fifie yawl	Dipping lugger	1906
Lord Roberts	Norfolk wherry	Wherry rig	1898
Madcap	Bristol Channel pilot cutter	Gaff cutter	1875
Margaret FY150	Mevagissey lugger	Dipping lugger	1903
Marguerite T	Bristol Channel pilot cutter	Gaff cutter	1893
Marion	Bristol Channel pilot cutter	Gaff cutter	1889
Maud (95)	Norfolk wherry	Wherry rig	1899
Nellie SU71	Solent smack	Gaff cutter	1865
Oigh Niseach	Ness sgoth	Dipping lugger	1980
Olga	Bristol Channel pilot cutter	Gaff cutter	1909
Olive (*95*, 95)	Norfolk wherry yacht	Wherry rig	1909
Peggy	Bristol Channel pilot cutter	Gaff cutter	1903
Pet IH45 (101, *103*)	Suffolk Beach Boat	Dipping lugger	1902
Pilot	Sheringham crabber	Lugger	1937

Reaper FR858	Fifie	Dipping lugger	1902
Research LK62	Zulu	Dipping lugger	1903
Sea Spray	Stonehaven Zulu skiff	Dipping lugger	
Spirit of Merseyside	Liverpool pilot schooner	Gaff schooner	1984
Spray WK1767	Findochty scaffie	Dipping lugger	1913
Sweet Promise	Hartlepool coble	Dipping lugger	1906
Tern	Stroma yawl	Dipping lugger	1870
Wendy Mary	Hastings beach boat	Dipping lugger	1951
White Moth	Wherry yacht	Wherry rig	1913
Winnie MN71	Winkle brig	Gaff sloop	1889
Wonder SU120	Solent smack	Gaff cutter	1860

English Smacks

In Britain the term smack was often used to cover any type of gaff-rigged fishing, pilot or passenger craft, but it is usually only applied to gaff-rigged fishing craft. There were many types of smack and many of these have been converted to yachts. The following list are those that have been kept to near original appearance.

name	number	type	place & date of building	
ADC (100)	CK431	Essex smack	Brightlingsea	1890
Alberta	CK318	Essex smack	Brightlingsea	1885
Ant	CK261	Essex smack	Brightlingsea	
Bertha	MN48	Essex smack	Brightlingsea	1887
Betty	CK145	Essex smack	Brightlingsea	1906
Boadicea (*83*, 99, 100)	CK213	Maldon smack	Maldon	1808
Bona	LO178	Leigh bawley	Brightlingsea	1903
Boy Eric		Lowestoft trawler	Rye	1921
Britannia		Wash smack	King's Lynn	1915
Charlotte Ellen (99, 100, *158*)	CK258	Essex smack	Brightlingsea	1906
Cleone		Ramsgate trawler	Sittingbourne	1920
Doris	LO20	Leigh bawley	Harwich	1912
Dorothy	CK159	Essex smack	Brightlingsea	1899
Ellen	CK222	Essex smack	Rowhedge	1900
Ethel Alice	CK476	Essex smack	Brightlingsea	1897
Excelsior	LT472	Lowestoft trawler	Lowestoft	1921
Fly	MN17	Essex smack		
Freda & Nora	BN154	Wash smack	King's Lynn	1912
Gamecock	F76	Whitstable oyster	Whitstable	1906
George & Alice	CK76	Essex smack	Brightlingsea	1909
Gracie (100)	CK46	Essex smack	Wivenhoe	1897
Gratitude		Trawler	Porthleven	1907
Grethe Witting (ex-*Nordford Suffling*)		Drifter	Lowestoft	1914
Harriet Blanche		Essex smack	Brightlingsea	1912

Helen & Violet	LO262	Leigh bawley	Harwich	1906
Horace & Hannah (101)		Yarmouth shrimper		1908
Hyacinth (100, *121*)	CK256	Essex oyster smack	Brightlingsea	1900
Ida	CK3	Essex smack	Brightlingsea	1876
Jim Morgan		Lowestoft trawler	Lowestoft	1881
Johanna		Grimsby trawler	Rye	1884
Joseph T	MN9	Maldon smack	Maldon	1901
Kate	CK139	Essex smack	Paglesham	1883
Katie	CK82	Essex smack	Brightlingsea	1889
Kenya Jacaranda	BM57	Brixham trawler	Brixham	1923
Leader		Brixham trawler	Galmpton	1892
Lilian		Gravesend bawley	Gravesend	1869
Lily May	LN230	Wash smack	King's Lynn	1912
Lizzie Annie	MN23	Essex smack	Brightlingsea	1903
Maria	CK21	Essex smack	Rowhedge	1866
Marigold	MN119	Bawley	Maldon	1981
Marita		Essex smack		
Martha Two	MN69	Essex smack	Brightlingsea	1876
Mary	CK252	Essex smack	Brightlingsea	1899
Mary Amelia		Leigh cockle boat	Southend	1914
Maud	MN21	Essex smack	Maldon	1876
Mayflower (100)	CK44	Essex smack	Brightlingsea	1887
Mermaid (*121*)	LN32	Wash smack	Boston	1904
Nellie & Leslie (106)		Wash smack	King's Lynn	1911
Ostrea Rose (85–86)	MN183	Maldon smack	Heybridge	1980
Peace	CK171	Essex smack	Brightlingsea	1909
Pembeth		Essex smack	Brightlingsea	1912
Phantom		Essex smack	Brightlingsea	1897
Polly	MN12	Essex smack	Maldon	1889
Priscilla	MN76	Essex smack	Brightlingsea	1893
Provident		Brixham trawler	Brixham	1924
Quiz (100)		Essex smack	Paglesham	1872
Regard		Brixham trawler yacht		1933
Rosa & Ada (*121*)	F105	Whitstable smack	Whitstable	1908
Rosena	CK65	Essex smack	Brightlingsea	1899
Sallie	CK224	Essex smack	Brightlingsea	1907
Saxonia	CK90	Bawley	Brightlingsea	1932
Shamrock	CK174	Essex smack	Brightlingsea	1900
Sir William Archibald		Mission smack	Gt Yarmouth	1928
Skylark		Essex smack	Brightlingsea	1905
Souvenir	LO5	Bawley	Maldon	1933
Speedwell		Whitstable smack	Burnham-on-Crouch	1909
Stormy Petrel (100)	F71	Whitstable smack	Whitstable	1890
Sunbeam (100)	CK328	Essex smack	Maldon	1881
Telegraph	BN122	Wash smack	Boston	1906
Thistle	RR2	Medway bawley	Strood	1887

OLD COLOUR FILM ON TV
(m NAUTY?)

Unity	*ON 1248*	Wash smack	Boston	c1900
Valkyrja		Essex smack	Brightlingsea	1896
Venture		Paull shrimper		1907
Victory	LO111	Essex smack	Maldon	1895
Vigilance		Brixham trawler	Brixham	1926
Westward Ho		Humber trawler	Grimsby	1888
William	MN15	Essex smack	Maldon	1889
William & Emily	CK212	Essex smack	Tollesbury	1886
William McCann		Humber trawler	Hull	1884
Yet		Essex smack	Brightlingsea	1908

A list of Falmouth (or Truro River) work boats can be found in *Living History Under Sail*, published by Falmouth Working Boats Association.

Getting the big jib in on *L'Atalanta* in the 1983 Stour Old Gaffers Race with the smack *Charlotte Ellen* still heading for the turning mark. *Author*

Organizations which help to keep traditional vessels sailing

American Marine Education Society
Gardner's Basin
Atlantic City
NJ 08401
USA

Association of Bargemen
5 Abbey Place
Faversham
Kent
UK

Cat Boat Association
10 Summer Street
Kingston

MA 02364
USA

China Clipper Society (Inca)
101 High Street
Lenham
Maidstone
Kent
UK

Colne Smack Preservation Society
c/o J Lawrence (sailmaker)
Tower Street
Brightlingsea
Colchester

Essex
UK

Dolphin Sailing Barge Museum
Crown Quay Lane
Sittingbourne
Kent
UK

Falmouth Working Boats Association
c/o J McDonald
Ferry Quay
23 Trefusis Road
Flushing
Falmouth
Cornwall
UK

**Foreningen far Bevaring av Eldre
Seilfartøyer**
(Norwegian Coast & Sail Society)
c/o Tryggen Larsen
Karl Johansgate 20
Oslo 1
Norway

Freunde des Gaffelriggs
(Friends of the Gaff Rig)
c/o Uwe P Griem
AM Rehm 25
207 Ahrensburg
Germany

Friendship Sloop Society
Friendship
ME 04547
USA

Galway Hookers Association
c/o P Barry
21 Belgrove Road
Blackrock
Co Dublin, Eire

General Superintendent (Scow schooner
Alma)
National Recreational Area
Fort Mason
San Francisco
CA 94123
USA

Groupe Finistèrien de Croisière
UDNF
Pors–Beac'h
29224 Logonna Daoulas
France

Heritage Boat Club
HBC 4420N
Maplewood
Chicago
IL 60625
USA

Het Varend Museumschip
(Sailing Museum Ship Society)
Herengracht 43
1398 JB Enkuizen
The Netherlands

**Humber Keel & Sloop Preservation
Society**
Glenlea
Main Road, New Ellerby
Hull HU11 5BT
UK

Humber Sailing Trawler Society
238 Beverley Road
Anlaby
East Yorkshire
England

Island Cruising Club
Island Street
Salcombe
Devon TQ8 8DR
England

Jubilee Sailing Trust
Atlantic Road
Eastern Docks
Southampton SO1 1GD
England

Kentish Sail Association
c/o L Tester
Hollow Shore
Faversham
Kent
England

Maine Windjammer Association
Box 317A
Rockport
ME 04856
USA

Mariners International Club
58 Woodville Rd
New Barnet
Herts EN5 SEG
England

Maritime Trust
16 Ebury Street
London SW1W 0LH
England

Mayflower Sail Training Society
Box 16
Europe House
World Trade Centre
London E1 9AA
England

Museumshafen Övelgönne
Övelgönne 42
2000 Hamburg 63
Germany

Mystic Seaport Museum
Mystic
CT 06355
USA

Norfolk Wherry Trust
c/o P Oakes
63 White Hall Road
Norwich,
Norfolk
England

North Devon Museum Trust
26 Fore Street
Northam
Bideford
Devon

Nova Scotia Schooner Association
c/o Lunenburg Yacht Club
Lunenburg
Nova Scotia
Canada

Ocean Research & Education Society
64 Commercial Wharf
Boston
MA 02025
USA

Old Gaffers' Association
c/o David Cade
Steps Cottage
Playden
Rye
East Sussex

Old Gaffers' Association (North America)
c/o Leonard G Kavanagh
88 Lenox Rd
Nahant
MA 01908
USA

Old Gaffers' Association (Western Australia)
c/o B Hicks
10 Jubilee Street
Beckenham 6107
Western Australia
Australia

Passmore Edwards Museum (owners of barge *Dawn)*
Romford Road
Stratford
London E15 4LZ
England

Ronde en Platbodem Jachten (Dutch Round and Flat Bottom Barge Yachts)
p/a P J Zaaijer
Kemplaan Io
8601 ZH Sneek
The Netherlands

Sailing Barge Association
Thamesia House
9 Wapping Lane
London E1 9DA
England

Sail Training Association
2A The Hard
Portsmouth
Hants PO1 3PT
England

Schiffergilde Bremerhaven (Skipper's Guild) **EV**
Van-Ronzelen-Strasse
2850 Bremerhaven M
Germany

Scottish Veteran & Vintage Fishing Vessel Club
Scottish Fisheries Museum
Harbour Head
Anstruther
Fife KY10 3AB
Scotland

Sea Cadet Association
Broadway House

The Broadway
London SW19 1RL
England

Seilskoyteklubber Colin Archer (Club)
Box 190
Sentrum
Oslo 1
Norway

Society for Spritsail Barge Research
c/o M A Farnham
21 Grasslands
Langley
Maidstone
Kent ME17 3JJ
England

Solent Smack Society
Wicormarine Ltd
Cranleigh Road
Portchester
Hampshire
England

Sveriges Segelfartygs (Swedish
Traditional Ship Association)
Box 22536
10422 Stockholm
Sweden

Thames Barge Sailing Club
c/o National Maritime Museum
Greenwich
London SE10
England

Traeskibs Sammenslutning
(Danish Wooden Ship Society)
Strandhøjsvej 7

3050 Humlebaek
Denmark

Vereniging Botterhound (Wooden
Fishing Boats of Ijsselmeer and
Waddenzee)
p/a G J Luijendijk
Coender Straat 1
2613 S M Delft
The Netherlands

Vieux Gréements de France
(French Old Gaffers Association)
7 Rue des Palombes
35650 Le Rheu
Rennes
France

West of Scotland Boat Museum
132 Harbour Street
Irvine
Ayrshire
Scotland

Westward Ho (Smack)
Debes Christiansen
v/ Landavegen
3800 Thorshavn
Faeroe Islands
Denmark

Windjammer for Hamburg
Steckelhorn 9
2000 Hamburg 11
Germany

Zeilvaart Enkhuizen (Dutch Charter
Vessels)
ZD Havendijk 101
1601 JB Enkhuizen
The Netherlands

The 74 gun ship of the line *Implacable* being sunk in the English Channel in 1949 by the Royal Navy. Built in 1789 as the French *Duguay Trouin*, she fought at the Battle of Trafalgar and was later captured by the British. Twenty years later a ship of this importance would have been preserved rather than scuttled.